Dismantling the Stigma:

10 Truths About ADHD

Micheal D. Woodruff

* * *

Dedication

To my sons, Jacob and Phillip (R.I.P.) . Had it not been for you, I doubt I would have ended up in a position to be tested. The testing and revelation of my own issues with ADHD, as well as the new awareness of the relationship between your ADHD and mine, is what lead to the research and writing of this book. Without knowing it, you've made this book possible.

I love you, Always.

Dad

Introduction:

First, let me thank you for picking up this book. It says at least two things about you. One, that you know about or have experienced the stigmas related to ADHD. Two, that you want to educate yourself and others on the realities behind ADHD and not rely solely on your own ideations.

Most people with ADHD have lived through the name calling, false classifications, and limitations of other's beliefs about them. Many of those same people didn't realize they even had ADHD and probably thought there was something wrong with them. They've listened to the stigmas and have often placed those stigmas on themselves.

Those who know someone with ADHD traits have likely fallen into the trap of believing the stigmas or even solidified their beliefs. Without knowing it, they contribute to the devastating mindset that people with ADHD suffer with every day.

This book was designed to approach things from a non-clinical perspective. I don't have a degree in any psychology but don't let that dissuade you from reading on. In the pages that follow, you'll find examples and clarifications that people with ADHD and those without often experience. This book was designed for those who want to know more about themselves, their friends, or their family. Some might be interested in discovering how it affects their coworkers, employees, and even their bosses.

This book isn't for everyone. This book is not for you if you prefer clinical terms, stale studies, or targeted reference material. If you want a casual conversation that leaves you a bit more enlightened and educated, read on.

By the time you finish reading this book, you'll have a much better understanding of the truth behind the stigmas. You'll be able to see things from a different perspective and, hopefully, you'll be able to improve your relationship with yourself and those around you.

It's time to stop living with the stigmas that have been so limiting for so long. It's time to get a better understanding of the truth of ADHD. It's time to stop putting restrictions on the capabilities of those with ADHD.

* * *

Interview with Kent Sanders

Kent Sanders, Ghostwriter, Host of the Daily Writer Podcast & The Profitable Writer membership, was asked about his experience with Attention Deficit Hyperactivity Disorder. Kent doesn't have ADHD himself and, like most people, only had a rudimentary knowledge of it.

People with ADHD have trouble focusing, constantly need to switch tasks, and have difficulty sitting still. "*That's my impression. I could be off base, but that's about my depth of knowledge.*"

As a professor for seventeen years, Kent has worked with many students who used IEPs (Individualized Education Programs) for different reasons. In that experience, he never considered ADHD to affect intelligence. "Everybody *has preferred ways of learning. Everybody's intelligent. They're just intelligent in different ways.*"

When asked about ADHD medication, the only one he knew of was Ritalin, and he believes that there is a sense that it has been over-prescribed. At least, that's the overall impression he's gotten based on what people have talked about.

At the time of the interview, Kent could only recall one person who talked about having ADHD. To his knowledge, he didn't know any women who had ADHD, and like most people, believed it to be a predominantly male diagnosis. The one person he knew off-hand was a fellow teacher who took medication. Kent believed it helped that person be a better teacher because he could sympathize with students who struggled with different learning issues.

When someone is struggling, the blanket solution is for that person to try harder–a mindset that Kent does not find helpful. "*To tell somebody to just do this differently or try harder doesn't really work. It minimizes the condition they have."* It's like telling a blind person to try harder and they'll be able to see. *"You're telling that person to change something that they can't. It's part of their makeup."* As someone who has struggled with depression his whole life, Kent understands that the idea of trying harder can make things worse. A person will try harder, but when they are unable to improve their situation, they feel worse about themselves.

The same goes for using punishment as a means to get someone to stop having ADHD. *"I don't think punishment is the best motivator. Plus, punishing somebody for something they can't help doesn't seem right."*

* * *

It's All About Discipline

A good kick in the pants will cure the "ADHD" problem.
"Tommy was always a problem child," said Elaine, his mother. "I could never get him to sit still for longer than five minutes. I thought that was the way all children were. I didn't give it much thought."

As Tommy got older, Elaine expected his attention span to improve. When he started school, things seemed to get worse. He was full of energy. "What boy isn't?" she said. "That's the way it is with boys. Right?" Not only was Tommy an active child, but he also preferred to be by himself. He only seemed interested in playing with the other children for a short time. He got bored with the games they played, or he would get angry when things didn't go the way he thought they should. As the years went on, Tommy's reactions worsened.

Tommy's mother struggled to control her son's behavior on a daily basis. He became more defiant and spent most of his time alone in his room. He would spend hours playing video games. He needed several reminders that it was time for dinner. When it came to his homework, she would have to force him to sit at the table to complete it. He would forget to do his chores, even though she listed them on a whiteboard where he could see them. She tried talking to him, but that never seemed to work. Everything went in one ear and out the other. He wouldn't even look at her when she was talking most of the time.

Desperate to find a solution, she talked with other parents about how they handle their kids. Some suggested that she needed to use a firm hand with the boy. She admitted that she didn't spank him. She never believed in corporal punishment. Others suggested the lack of discipline allows her son to act like he does. "A boy needs to know who's in charge." They'd say.

Some pointed to a less physical approach. They told her, "He needs to understand what he's doing wrong." Elaine admitted that she tried to explain why Tommy shouldn't act as he did, but he claimed he couldn't help it. She tried to understand but always believed that everyone can control how they act. He was choosing to be defiant, disruptive, and dangerous. It had to stop. Tommy's mother decided to temper the two. She would try a combination of physical intervention and verbal correction.

Regarding homework, she didn't sit with him as often. Instead, she allowed him to make his own decision to stay. When he didn't, she'd yell at him to get back to the table. If he couldn't do his homework with the same focus he had while playing video games, then he would fail school. She told him being stupid would keep him back, and he'd have to watch all his friends move on without him. She'd tell him that having an idiot son wasn't something she signed up for when she became a mother.

Reminding him that he was getting dumber every day made him more reclusive. When she yelled at him, his eyes would gloss over, and he would stare at nothing. Determined to keep his attention, Elaine turned to physical measures. A smack here and there now and again. If he forgot to do his chores, she'd pop him on the back of the head or on the arm and take away his game time. She scolded him for being irresponsible and demanded he do more to help. She was his mother, not his maid, and he needed to do more.

Over time, Tommy's mother became accustomed to yelling at him. He got used to getting smacked on the arm, back, and head for no reason. If he looked confused, she would tell him he knew what it was for. Sometimes, she would point to the list of chores. If she raised her hand to hit him again, he scrambled to do what he thought she wanted. Tommy believed he couldn't do anything right.

When he sat down to watch television, he waited for the yelling and the hitting to start. He flinched when she entered the room and wondered what she would yell at him for next.

He was afraid to play games and hid his phone when he heard her coming. School became his only refuge, but his grades started to drop. He stopped bringing his assignments home and told her he had no homework. She never checked. She only wanted him to behave. It was all she could hope for.

Tommy stopped doing anything that would allow his mother or anyone else to judge him. He stopped playing sports, even catch, because he was afraid to make a mistake. Any mistake meant that she would ridicule and punish him. His mother's frustration grew as his grades got worse. The less he got involved, the more aggressive she became. Discipline became abuse.

Tired of his mother's hatred, Tommy figured the best way to make her happy was to run away.

Getting crumbs out of a toaster

Remember those old toasters with only one or two slots for bread? The vertical kind, not the toaster oven style. Believe it or not, you can still buy that style. They're great when you want toast or a toasted bagel without changing the settings. Put the bread in and push down on the lever. Simple. Except there was a problem. The toasters collected crumbs.

As time passed, they added an easy way to get the crumbs out. A panel on the bottom flipped open and out dropped the excess bread crumbs. Convenient, right? Most of the time, yes. Weekly or monthly cleaning, and you didn't have to worry about your toaster catching on fire—a great preventive measure. Before the introduction of the crumb panel, you had to tip the toaster over and give it a few good whacks.

In the old days, whacks were a common thing. When the television wasn't working right, a good thump or two on the side fixed the issue. Having a problem with your carburetor? A simple whack with a hammer could solve the short-term problem. Window air conditioning unit acting up? Well, you get the idea. A good whack was the cure for many problems back in the day. You still might catch yourself, or someone you know, using the Whack-Fix method.

With modern technology, the Whack-Fix method is ill-advised. Giving your iPhone a good whack will only give your screen a good crack. Too hard of a bump against your LED Smart TV, and you'll have to buy a new one. Don't even think about taking a hammer to your modern car. Things don't work that way anymore.

The tendency to use physical force is still a strong part of who we are as human beings. Ever assemble furniture? The desk should look one way, but it's impossible with the parts you have left. No problem; a hammer will force those two pieces together.

And there's always the drill option. Glue works, too. So what if it says all you need is a Phillips-head screwdriver? They never had to put it together themselves. Instructions? Those are the last resort for most people. When you finally decide to read them, you find out you were using the wrong part the whole time.

Now you have to choose. Undo what you've worked so hard on, or continue to force it into some new rearranged version of what you wanted. Beat on it long enough, and everything will turn out fine.

Children are not toasters

Of course, children aren't toasters. It seems obvious, like an obvious statement, yet when you stop to think about it, they are often treated like they are. A good whack to clear their heads and make them pay attention. A few good whacks to get the cobwebs out of their head. A few more whacks to make them think about what they did wrong.

There was a time when most parents and caregivers used the Whack-Fix method on children. An occasional tap on the arm to redirect their attention is one thing. When it becomes forceful, painful, and repetitive, it becomes a problem. And the issue isn't with the child.

You know the scene. Dad takes his belt off and has a scowl on his face. The child knows what's coming. Survival instincts kick in, and the child scrambles to get away. The swinging starts. Legs. Face. Arms. Back. It didn't matter where the belt struck as long as the sting was there. There was a lesson to learn, and the belt would teach it. The lesson learned was simple. Stop being you.

The awareness of child abuse increased over the years. Child abuse cases have gone down because of it.

* 2016: 671,176 reported cases

* 2019: 656,251

* 2021: 618,399

A considerable drop over the years, but still too many. Those are also only the ones reported.

Neurodivergent children can be difficult to understand sometimes. It's important to realize that children with ADHD don't process information the same way. Ignoring those differences can lead to more frustration for everyone involved. That frustration gives way to emotional outbursts that can become abusive.

Diagnosing ADHD takes time. The stigma around ADHD might prevent a parent from having their child tested. It becomes either an avoidance issue or a denial. Parents see their child's unusual behavior as deliberate.

Sir Alexander Crichton recorded the symptoms of what is now called ADHD back in 1798. "Hyperkinetic Reaction of Childhood" was the original name for it. In 1902, British pediatrician Sir George Frederic Still used the term ADHD. The known history of the condition goes back for centuries, yet there are still those who deny it.

We learned to behave ourselves. Not paying attention wasn't an option. We were responsible for our behavior.

No excuses. Psychologists made it up for parents who want to be friends with their young.

Learned behavior came through corporal punishment and then passed down through the generations. Ever wonder why some children seemed to be in trouble all the time? Their struggle went untreated, and they learned how to force their will on others. They deny the existence of ADHD for fear of being wrong. They learned how to control themselves through self-demeaning thoughts and actions. Those "teaching" methods continued, getting worse over time.

Neurotypical children connect a disciplinary action with a behavior. ADHD children connect disciplinary action with existence. If the discipline is not connected to the action right away, the connection can get lost. The message to stop being who they are becomes etched in their memories.

Message received

Before the mid-eighties, corporal punishment for children was commonplace, at home, school, and even daycare. It was normal for the principal to have a paddle hanging on the wall behind their desk. It served as a reminder to students of what would happen if they got out of line.

Parents often had their favorite tool as well. Depending on your upbringing, it could have been a "switch," a belt, a cooking utensil, or a flip-flop. Some parents grabbed the first thing available.

There is a time and place for discipline. There is also a line between discipline and abuse, even if some see it as the same thing. There is no "one size fits all" form of discipline when it comes to raising children.

Some children are more receptive to a lecture than they are to a physical encounter. Some forms of punishment can come as added chores or time facing a wall. It could be a restriction on electronics. Finding the correct form of discipline can be difficult. When you love your child, you'll spend the time looking.

Discipline: The practice of training people to obey rules or a code of behavior.

How a child responds can show whether the form of discipline is effective. Do they understand the reason for the discipline? Was it for behavior or because they exist? Discipline without love destroys any positive view a child has about themselves. For children with ADHD, the message about themselves becomes clear.

Unwanted.

Unloved.

Always wrong.

The feelings they have about themselves turn into destructive actions.

Children with ADHD tend to cluster things together. Part of that has to do with limited working memory. To keep up with everything going on, the brain will group as much information as possible. Over time, they come to believe that their existence is the problem. If they want to avoid punishment, they need to make themselves scarce.

Other children will have the opposite reaction. They see that by acting in certain ways, they will get attention—any attention is better than no attention. Over time, this becomes the primary message: Act bad, and people will notice you. When people notice you, you matter. If no one notices you, you don't matter.

There is also the time difference between a behavior and a disciplinary action. For an NT child, referring back to what they did wrong is enough for them. The connection is easy to follow.

For an ND child, things aren't that straightforward. A hundred actions had transpired before the discipline occurred. What was it that they did wrong? All they could conclude was that the punishment was for existing.

Children with ADHD are more likely to receive disciplinary action. They grow up suffering from depression and anger management issues. Their childhood was about how they shouldn't have existed, not how they shouldn't have done something.

Punishment is not a cure

*"I don't think punishment is the best motivator. Plus, punishing somebody for something they can't help doesn't seem right."*Kent Sanders

A few swats on the behind during a child's impressionable years and the threat of ADHD will be gone forever. After all, it's a made-up thing so people can get away with bad behavior. All it takes is a firm hand. The same goes for any so-called handicap. They need to learn how to be obedient.

As ridiculous as it sounds, there are people who believe it. If that were the case, they would include techniques in pregnancy books. You would see them in every parenting periodical. If it worked for every potential problem a person might have, there wouldn't be any problems for long.

The denial of ADHD isn't anything new. Despite being shown in the DSM (American Psychiatric Association's Diagnostic and Statistical Manual of Mental Disorders) in 1968, people are still very ignorant of the subject.

Most people believe that psychiatric professionals made up the terms. It was a money-making, excuse-offering tool for brainwashing and controlling children. All children need is some discipline. Behavior is always a choice. Symptoms like being rambunctious, speaking out of turn, and doing random things at random times are acts of defiance. The problem with that line of thinking is that the child is acting on impulse. It's not a conscious thought to not sit still. They don't interrupt to be rude. A thought crosses their mind and they have to say it. Everything catches their interest, so they'll jump from one thing to another. It's not defiance. It's the way they're wired. They can't give you an explanation no matter how much you demand one.

When pressed for a reason, the child would make something up or tell you what they think you want to hear. Over time, their minds become programmed to those responses and false reasoning.

No one wants to have ADHD. No one wants their child to have ADHD. It's a world of mental and emotional complications. Reality seldom cares what someone wants. The best thing to do is to learn more about the issues and how to deal with them. No amount of punishment is going to cure someone of ADHD. It's frustrating for parents, and it's frustrating for the child. They struggle with why they act the way they do.

There's also a disconnect between behavior and discipline. That's not to encourage a lack of discipline. There are rules for a reason. ADHD doesn't give a free pass. Discipline should include patience, understanding, and explanation.

The Whack-Fix method may have worked on the old television set. It may get the crumbs out of the toaster. It seldom, if ever, has a positive impact on children. Humans are much more complex than simple machinery.

Understanding a child with ADHD means letting go of preconceived ideas. It means being willing to learn more about how your child processes information and stimulation.

* * *

You Need Self Control

Some people believe anyone who takes ADHD medication is avoiding self-control. If they learned how to take charge of their behavior, they wouldn't need the medication. After all, medication is a means of escaping responsibility and reality.

They don't accept that taking those medications helps those with ADHD regulate their lives. It allows them the ability to focus and maintain their self-control.

A neurotypical (NT) person usually only sees the negative impact medications have on people. Their focus is on the drug overdoses, addictions, and depression that results in suicide. They see some medicines being used for the wrong reasons. The conclusion is anyone who takes that kind of medicine has an addiction. They compare it to street drugs and painkillers. Even with generic painkillers, the resulting reactions vary from person to person. For them, the obvious solution is to stop taking the pills.

Neurodivergent (ND) people use medications to regulate their lives. The addiction that NDs have is to functionality, not an aversion to reality. Medication doesn't affect NDs the way it does NTs . There's an idea that the same medication affects everyone the same way. "Take two of these and call me in the morning" might work for a low-dose painkiller but not for guanfacine.

The need for certain types of medication varies from person to person, as does the dosage required. When someone takes pain medication when there is no pain, the results might give them a sense of euphoria. When someone takes ADHD medication but isn't neurodivergent, their behavior can become worse. Addictions occur when someone takes medication outside its intended use.

* * *

Finding the right medication can be daunting

Neurological medications aren't like painkillers. When you have a headache or are sore from over-exertion, it's usually recommended to take a couple of over-the-counter medicines. Acetaminophen, Ibuprofen, naproxen, or Aspirin are the most common.

Your typical NSAID (Non-Steroidal Anti-Inflammatory Drug) can be bought just about anywhere and affects most people the same way. They work to reduce swelling, lower fevers, and alleviate pain. The dosage may vary for effectiveness, but the process and results remain the same for just about everyone.

When it comes to neurological medications, a simple OTC (Over-the-counter) is not going to work. You can't go to your local drugstore and pick up a bottle of Alprazolam when you're feeling stressed. You can pick up some stress-relieving medications like Kava-Kava or Ashwagandha, but those aren't the same. Xanax doesn't have a one-size-fits-all prescription, nor does it have the same desired effect on everyone. Those with other neurological conditions may have adverse effects, and other medications would have to be considered.

Multiple medications are prescribed for people with ADHD, and it often takes a while to find the right medication and dosage. The trial and error process can take weeks or even months before there are positive results. In some cases, things get worse before they get better.

This is one of the reasons there is a stigma around ADHD meds. People only see the negative results. When the right dosage and combinations are found, one of the first things outsiders assume is that you've stopped taking the drugs.

"You're doing better. Did the doctor take you off those drugs that were messing you up?"

"No, I'm still taking the same ones, just a different dose."

"And you're doing okay?"

"Yeah, I'm doing great, actually."

"Oh."

Because of their belief that certain drugs make everyone behave the same way, it can be difficult for them to believe that those drugs can have any positive impact. They will tell you stories they heard about someone who was on a particular medication and all these bad things happened, and either things got better when they stopped taking it, or it ended in tragedy when they didn't. The horror stories are easy to find and imagine. The truth behind those stories is often ignored and untold. There's more to it than just the medication.

There's a process when it comes to finding the right medication for any type of mental disorder. Whether the issue is depression, anxiety, ADHD, Autism, PTSD, PNES, Schizophrenia, or bipolar disorder (and there are a lot more), there is a general starting point, but the modifications can be ongoing. The medication could be a short-term or long-term situation, and each one has complications of its own. Being wary of the possible side effects is a major concern. The other is obtaining the medication itself.

The ordeal of finding the right medication involves finding the right diagnosis. That cannot be done in a single office visit with a psychiatrist. It takes several visits, lots of questions, journals (which can be very insightful for them), and many other factors that come with making a diagnosis. Many times, additional attributes are considered, and medications can change. Regardless of what medication is found to work, obtaining those medications isn't easy.

ADHD and other ND medications are highly regulated. A prescription is required, and the counts are limited. Usually, it is thirty days, though on some occasions, exceptions are made for up to ninety days. That's it. Now, you might think that a ninety-day supply should be more than enough. Who needs to take something for that long anyway? If it were pain medication or antibiotics, you'd be right. Most of those are required only for a short period. That's not the case here. These medications become part of the daily routine so the person can have a daily routine.

If someone who is on ND medication moves and has to change doctors, there can be a lot of resistance to continuing the medicines. Every doctor believes they know better, and when going to a new doctor, they want to do their own evaluations while they wait for your medical records. These days, it can go a lot faster with digital documents, but even then, there will be resistance. Going to a new pharmacy adds to the stress, and then there is the cost.

ND medications aren't cheap. Even when covered by insurance, the cost can go into the high double digits. Without insurance, it can be in the hundreds or even thousands each month. The decision to get the medication could mean choosing between it and the rent. Going off the meds can lead to internal and external turmoil. Turning your life upside down, sideways, and blender setting Puree.

Just as there are multiple facets to the human psyche and neurological makeup, multiple medications may be required to aid the individual. When one medication becomes ineffective, unless the dose is exceptionally high, doctors will combine it with something else. It may take more than two combinations before positive changes are seen. Now, the patient is dealing with even more costs, more roadblocks, and more complications. That's not to say the combination isn't necessary. In many cases, they are. However, the impact on the individual's life becomes greater.

Dealing with the costs involved, the repeated dealings with new doctors, and trying to maintain some semblance of normalcy can add to the stress and anxiety of the neurodivergent person. The choice between rent or meds creates scenarios in the person's mind that can span months and even years. It becomes a downward spiral that accelerates as more details of their choices become apparent.

Some don't or won't understand the necessity of the medication. They view things through a distorted pair of binoculars from some far-away vantage point and are quick to make assumptions. One assumption is that the reason a person who no longer has access to their medication becomes so erratically different is because of withdrawals. But that's only part of the reason.

The withdrawals from recreational drugs usually pass within a few hours, days, or weeks. After that time, the person can begin to function normally, depending on the severity of the drugs they were using and the duration. For people who require proper medications to function, the process is considerably different. The reason they were on the medication in the first place is because of the way their brains process information and emotions.

The medications help regulate those processes similarly to how the brakes and accelerator regulate the speed of your car. When you alter or remove those regulations, you lose control, and bad things can happen. You might be able to maintain some control for a short time, but it becomes more and more difficult the longer you drive without them. If you're on a flat straight-away with no traffic, there aren't many obstacles to consider. If a turn is coming up, traffic is impeding the road, or bad weather is interfering with visibility, things can get dangerous real quick.

It's not much different for people with ADHD and other neurodivergent qualities. As long as things are going smoothly, the need for the medication may not be apparent. However, when life happens, which is very seldom a smooth road, having those regulating medications can make the difference between being able to navigate situations and ramming through them without control.

The withdrawal symptoms aren't the same as with a drug addict, nor is the time involved. When the body has worked through the medication in the system, it has effectively removed the metaphorical brake and acceleration aspects of the brain.

May contain side effects

Listening to drug commercials, you'll hear them list some of the possible side effects. If you listen to those side effects carefully, you might think twice about taking them. You have to weigh the risk against the reward.

"Side effects may include leprosy" - Nasal Spray

"Well, my nose fell off, but my sinuses are clearer than ever."

While that may be an extreme satirical example, in some cases, it's not too far off. How many medication commercials have you heard that list "possible death" or "may lead to death" as one of the side effects? Do you want to risk your life for something that may make your situation better? As with any medication consideration, you must weigh the pros and the cons.

- May Cause Skin Irritation or Discoloration
- Sleep Problems
- Anxiety
- Fatigue
- Upset Stomach
- Dizziness
- Dry Mouth
- Liver Damage
- Higher risk of suicide in adults ages 18-24
- Crankiness
- Behavior Problems
- Low Blood pressure— Suddenly stopping this medicine can result in high blood pressure
- Tiredness
- Sleepiness
- Nausea
- Vomiting
- Sleeplessness

- Irritability
- Headaches
- May make you more likely to have seizures
- Risk of heart arrhythmias

The list of side effects is from multiple ADHD medications, many of which list the same things. For the person with ADHD, they have to determine if the risk is worth the reward. In addition, finding the right dosage increases the odds of the side effects becoming severe.

While some may have a low-risk, high-reward ratio, the opposite can also be true. Some medications may be low risk but offer little benefit, while others may be highly beneficial but have dire side effects. The decision to take and continue taking neurodivergent medication isn't an easy one to make. The process can make a person wonder if it is worth it.

Hearing the stigma people place on ADHD medication can hinder their decision and cause them to remain in a perpetual state of inconsistency and sometimes harm. They don't want to become what the stigma claims they will.

Even after being on medications, adaptive factors come into play. The medication can become less effective over time, and new medications may be necessary. The decision process begins once again. It may be an ordeal the neurodivergent has gone through many times, but that doesn't mean it gets any easier. In many cases, it can be more difficult because they have finally found a way to regulate their lives, and someone shook the snow globe of their existence.

Euphoria or regulation

Back to the issue of recreational drug use versus necessary medication. Part of the brain is chemical, and part of it is electrical. There are a lot of complex particles and responses. Neurons and synapses. And a whole lot more. Not all chemical combinations, brain or medicinal, work the same way.

There's a process to mixing chemicals. First-year chemistry class should have taught you that. Mix the wrong chemicals and there will be a mess to clean up. Mix the right ones, and you created a new line of toothpaste.

The neurodivergent brain has a different chemical composition than a neurotypical brain. Even among neurodivergents, there are higher levels of some chemicals than others. The production of dopamine, for example, may be high in one person and almost non-existent in another. The right medication helps regulate the chemical balance. It allows that person to function in a way that will enable them to thrive rather than settle on surviving. There isn't a "high" connected to the medication.

It's easy to see only the negative impact of ADHD medications. The process of finding the right medication combination is sometimes daunting. The complications are, on occasion, horrific. It might feel like a living nightmare. Other experiences can be pleasant, if not mind-numbing. It is important to maintain the routine with the right combination.

A neurotypical person can take the same medications and have different results. They may experience euphoria or a bad trip. Or they might get a slight buzz. The recreational use of non-prescribed medication helps them escape reality. Those medications help the neurodivergent navigate their world.

* * *

All Boys Are Like That

Interview with Nathan Whitbread

The Neurodivergent Coach - https://theneurodivergentcoach.co.uk/

I had the great opportunity to speak with Nathan Whitbread, a neurodivergent coach for over seven years. He uses assistive technology like Dragon Natural Speak, Mind Mapping, and others to help those struggling with neurodivergent situations. He says, *"It's not the technology that solves the problem; it's the processes that solve the problem."*

In his years working with neurodivergents from all walks of life, he offered some insights and experience with ADHD beliefs. Some of the stigmas he's encountered are that boys, typically, are branded at a young age. They're seen as naughty, disruptive, and bossy.

> *"As a child, because of the way they work stuff out, there's a distorted perception. Instead of trying to engage with the person, you're engaging with the behavior and not recognizing what's really going on."*

> The impact leans more heavily toward boys than girls. *"There's definitely underdiagnosis amongst females. The traits are still for females as they are for men."*

He mentions that, when it comes to productivity, many people only see the peaks or valleys. The cycles themselves often go unseen. What a person witnesses in that cycle makes a determination in their minds about people with ADHD in general. Either they're highly productive or non-productive. They take that limited perception and apply it to the whole, often without thinking about it.

In his experience, he observed that some of the young people he knew growing up who had an ADHD diagnosis were full of huge amounts of energy, and often were very over-excitable. Through his own experiences with people, how they react, and how his mind works, Nathan has learned that he should apologize for who he is, though it is important to be clear about why he behaves the way he does. He understands it can be very frustrating for loved ones who get caught up in seemingly random behavior.

Nathan recognized that his own ADHD traits help with his creativity and enthusiasm. The downside is that it can often leave people behind.

> *I think my ADHD traits really help with creativity, drive, and enthusiasm. But what they also mean is they can leave people behind and make them feel that they've not been listened to and that I don't value their opinion just because my brain is racing so fast. This is not to excuse that, but I think it's key to recognize it and then work out how to help people understand that they are important and what they have to say is important.*

If given the opportunity to send a message to someone who shows ADHD traits but has not yet been diagnosed, he had this to say:

> *Focus on who you are and what you're good at. Make sure you write it down. Recognize the things that you find difficult and write them down, too. Think about your energy in terms of when you have good energy during the day and when you are likely to be depleted because of sleep or whatever else is going on. Then, based on that, make decisions about how you want to spend your time and when you want to do your best stuff.*

> *The key thing here is to be kind to yourself. Recognize that ADHD manifests itself differently in each individual because of the intersection of who we are. What's important is that we are true to ourselves and that we are the best version of ourselves. Do not*

be afraid to ask questions, but always treat all information with healthy skepticism and work out if it is relevant or useful to you.

They all have a little ADHD

Here's a thought: why don't we dispel the myth of all boys having ADHD? It simply isn't true. Most boys are active, true enough, but that doesn't mean they need to be put on medication. How about letting them run around outside longer? Get them off the video games, social media, and streaming services for a while. Odds are they'll burn off that excess energy that interferes with their focus. They won't be as fidgety. They might even improve their grades and social skills.

For the boys who do have ADHD, the manifestation will become easier to recognize. Their tendency to fidget, drift, lose focus, and other ADHD attributes won't wear off. It's dangerous to assume all boys have Attention Deficit Hyperactivity Disorder. Those that do get ignored while those that don't end up as mindless drones. Both end up paying the price.

Such beliefs dismiss the struggles ADHD'ers deal with on a daily, and sometimes hourly, basis. It increases their Rejection Sensitivity Dysphoria (RSD). Their depression worsens. Their ability to focus and function decreases. Their overall quality of life suffers because now they believe they are truly defective. Other boys are doing fine with their ADHD; why can't I?

Why this stigma? It could have something to do with the name. "Attention Deficit" is the first part people notice. It's a constant fight to get the child's attention. It's as if they don't care. People fail to remember how boys, especially younger ones, have an insatiable curiosity. Everything grabs their attention. They want to know more, but not necessarily what you're trying to teach.

The next part, Hyperactivity, is the most talked about. Since boys naturally have a lot of energy, they're bound to be hyper. Boys, in general, tend to be more physically active than girls, and so, by that comparison, boys have ADHD and girls don't. It also leads to the misconception that ADHD is something a person grows out of because most males settle down as the years pass.

With the idea that all boys have ADHD and, at some point, they'll grow out of it, comes the idea that there's nothing to be done except a little more discipline. Beyond that, the mentality remains that "Boys will be boys." With that mindset, the children who need help don't receive it but get penalized for how their mind works.

Hyperactivity isn't only about the obvious inability to sit still. In my case, I was forced to sit still or face punishment, which resulted in my inability to relax at all.

Not neurologically.

Not mentally.

Not physically.

People use various methods to relax their bodies and minds. None of them have worked for me. "Breathe in - breathe out" increases my anxiety levels. It's more than being fidgety. There's an underlying current that constantly shifts the way my body reacts. Even when I'm asleep, my brain runs full throttle, playing dreams in ultra-dynamic, semi-interactive, full-color extreme vision.

In school, I often leaned my chair back and hit my head against the wall. Part of me was bored. Part of me needed the movement. Part of me appreciated it when I stopped. It wasn't because I was a boy. It was because of my undiagnosed ADHD. If it were just the constant physical movement and an attempt to stifle the hyperactivity, the dismissal might be understandable. Every boy with hyperactive tendencies doesn't go through the other issues ADHD brings on.

When the mind is in a constant thought version of thermal runaway, emotions will try to step in to offer some regulation. The problem is, most of the time, those emotions start in a neutral state and slide faster and faster toward a depressive state. For me, the feeling of being happy doesn't exist. For a very long time, I thought that being happy was something people made up. I learned to mimic being happy, but I could never feel it. That's not to say I've never been grateful, but being happy always eluded me.

I had, and sometimes still have, difficulty regulating my emotions. I know what I'm supposed to feel at different times, but I don't. Other times,I'll have emotional outbursts that don't fit the apparent situation. My emotional state can go from being moderate to extreme sadness and then outright anger. It'll drop to depression in the blink of an eye.

Over time, I learned that emotions were something I was not allowed to have. Emotional dysregulation is another aspect of ADHD and isn't something all boys struggle with.

I Forgot

Doing a quick search for "memory tricks," I received about 171,000,000 results (0.39 seconds)—everything from mnemonics to chunking to writing things down. The easiest one, paying attention, is likely the most difficult for the neurodivergent. If something isn't interesting or done automatically, it doesn't get placed in any memory slot. It's done in the subconscious and relies on muscle memory. If it's not interesting, it might not get that much attention.

Everyone forgets things from time to time. Usually, when it's something they're not interested in or paying attention to. There are a myriad of memory techniques that can help people remember lists, names, and even the periodic table. Struggles with memory are a part of most people's lives. My mother used to say that my two favorite words were "I forgot" and "I don't know." I lost count of how many times I wanted to correct her about how many words they actually were.

It wasn't so much that I forgot things as it was that I didn't process the information in the first place. Unless it was pertinent and repeated, the information slid out of my mind like duck off a water's back.

My working memory was, and is, limited. I have to take steps to retain the information that allows me to process it into long-term memory. If I don't write something down, I'm likely to not have any recollection of it five minutes later. I also use other memory techniques that allow my limited working memory to file things in a different format. Often an MP4, GIF, or JPEG as computer comparatives go.

Memorization takes time and repetition. Working memory doesn't. There are certain numbers of slots for working memory. If the average person has six memory slots, the person with ADHD might only have three. The information in those memory slots is constantly being changed out. It makes remembering things in the short term more difficult and frustrating.

The problem with limited working memory is another sign that ADHD may be an issue. It's not about being inattentive, usually, but rather there being a problem with working memory. Some people with ADHD have found ways that work for them to override the working memory problem. That doesn't mean the issue isn't there. It just means they've figured out how to reroute the information.

In times of stress or sudden changes in routine, that process becomes disrupted, and they have to work hard to get things back in alignment. In the meantime, their working memory tries to take over and things don't work out so well.

Not all boys have ADHD

When someone thinks about ADHD, odds are they picture a boy. Probably a redhead unless they know someone personally. It's almost always a boy, and with it comes the idea that if ADHD was a real thing, which many still believe is made up, it's something that all boys have. The diagnostic statistics show that boys are more likely to be diagnosed with ADHD than girls. Since boys are more often diagnosed with ADHD, the belief is enforced that all boys have ADHD.

However, the overall percentage of children, boys (15%) and girls (7%), that are diagnosed with ADHD is somewhere around 11%, according to the National Institute of Mental Health (2011). When you look at the numbers, it is clear that not all boys have ADHD. Even if the numbers only represent half of the total to include undiagnosed cases, it's a long way from everyone having ADHD. If that were the case, they would be neurotypical rather than neurodivergent. The vast majority of boys don't have ADHD, nor is there a reason to suspect that they do. For many children, it's just a matter of excess energy.

It might be a phase

Children are, for the most part, always on the go. As one saying goes, "Youth is wasted on the young." If we could somehow harness the energy of youth, we could power cities for centuries. There's a natural exuberance that comes with youthfulness that dwindles over time.

Most children are easily distracted, have difficulty listening, and usually don't do things exactly as you instructed. It's pretty normal and doesn't necessarily mean the child has ADHD. Deciding that it is or isn't ADHD shouldn't be done in a singular season. Time is often the deciding factor. Their behavior may be different in the summer than in the winter.

There are patterns of behavior to look for and questions to ask.

- Is the child constantly fidgeting, even during times of quiet and rest?

- Do you repeatedly have to get their attention when talking to them?

- Do they tend to jump from one activity to another?

- Are they constantly losing things?

- Do they get bored easily?

- Are they disorganized even after everything has been organized for them?

- Has this behavior been going on for longer than six months?

This isn't an exhaustive or diagnostic list by any means, but they are questions that should be considered. If the majority of the time the answer is occasionally, then your child is probably just energetic.

However, if the answer is a resounding yes to most of these and other questions, it may be a good idea to talk to a professional who understands ADHD. It is even better if they specialize in neurodivergent conditions. Before concluding whether they do or do not have ADHD, speaking with a professional could make a huge impact on your child's future. Just as there is an inherent danger in assuming it's merely a phase, there's also a danger in unnecessarily medicating a child who doesn't have ADHD.

A child that has ADHD but doesn't get the help they need will spend a lot of time trying to figure out why they can't get things right. They may berate themselves for their mistakes and believe the people who say they're not trying hard enough.

To believe and express that "All boys have ADHD" is to disregard the struggles of the ones who actually do have ADHD. It denies them the help they need to regulate their behaviors and thought patterns. It tells them that any problems they have are purely their fault. It diminishes their plight and lets them know you believe they are inadequate. This only feeds the depressive thoughts that form in their minds and digs into their subconscious. Over the years, those seeds grow into dangerous thoughts and actions.

ADHD isn't something to fear

There have been, and still are, plenty of parents who don't want their child to be labeled as having ADHD. They don't want their child to be labeled as Autistic. They don't want their child to be labeled as anything that may have a negative implication. They don't want their child to be an embarrassment to them. Other parents might keep their kids away if they hear your child has a mental disorder.

There's an odd belief that ADHD, Autism, or any other neurodivergent condition is something that can be spread through contact. It's an irrational fear, and feeding that fear doesn't do anyone any good. In fact, it does further harm because the child has to figure out ways to appear normal, hide any behavior or thought that is disapproved of, all while struggling to figure out why they're not like everyone else. They see people's reactions and wonder why they are so defective. The struggle becomes destructive and follows them well into adulthood.

If there are signs and concerns that ADHD may be a factor, don't be afraid to have some testing done. Testing for ADHD isn't something your local general practitioner can do, but they may be able to point you in the right direction. Ask for a referral to a reputable psychologist who deals with ADHD. Take the matter seriously, but don't treat it like an armed weapon of mass destruction, either.

Some things can help your child function in a world that can be overwhelming, overstimulating, and boring at the same time. Their minds may not function like yours, and they may not see things the way you do. The help they can receive if they have ADHD, or if they classify as neurodivergent, can change their lives (and yours) for the better.

ADHD doesn't care about XX or XY chromosomes. Not all boys have ADHD. Some girls do. It doesn't manifest the same way in all cases and can vary greatly from person to person. There are feminine and masculine attributes to ADHD that can appear in girls and boys. It's not easy to identify, but that doesn't mean it should be dismissed or feared.

Learning more about ADHD in children and adults, regardless of sex, is an ongoing process. Professionals who deal with it regularly are valuable resources of help and can offer multiple treatment options.

ADHD directly impacts millions of people. Millions more are affected indirectly by untreated or unregulated ADHD. The effect may not be obvious, but it's there nonetheless. It should not be dismissed as an "every boy" type of thing. Those who do have it will need help from people who care enough to see them for who they are.

* * *

You're Lazy

Interview with Nick Pavlidis

Nick Pavlidis is a former corporate and bankruptcy litigation lawyer who works full-time as a ghostwriter for CEOs, thought leaders, and entrepreneurs. Nick was diagnosed with ADHD at thirty-six years old. His ADHD went unnoticed for the early part of his life because he managed to adapt himself to his surroundings.

I had been very productive and successful but was always finding it difficult to concentrate, sit still, and follow through on tasks outside of work settings. Even in the work setting, if a task was administrative or not very mission-driven, I found it difficult to complete those tasks.

During the first decade of his career, he had a support staff to handle the tasks he found difficult to concentrate on. It wasn't until he switched from a large law firm in New York City to a smaller corporate environment that his symptoms became more noticeable.

I had much less administrative support; I began to experience quite a bit of frustration.

Through his wife's encouragement, Nick decided to talk to someone about it and see what help might be available.

After a few days of testing, I was diagnosed as having ADHD.

So why wasn't Nick diagnosed early on?

Unfortunately, I don't have many childhood memories because I was in a serious accident during my senior year of high school. From what I understand, though, I was constantly getting in trouble for being talkative, disruptive, and antsy in school.

According to his understanding of his childhood, the traits were there, but like many in his generation, they were likely ignored for one reason or another. The confusing signals of whether he was lazy or an extremely hard worker were dependent on the tasks he was assigned to complete.

I have also been called both lazy and an extremely hard worker, both at work and in my personal life. Looking back, there has been a clear distinction between when I'd be called lazy and when I'd be called hard-working. When something isn't very mission-driven or purposeful, I find it hard to get motivated. When there's a big purpose to a task that's greater than myself, there's very little that can stop me.

For Nick, the purpose of the task made the difference between being "lazy" and being "hard-working," The level of purposefulness engaged his motivation. The stigmas others have had about Nick haven't stopped him from looking at things with a positive view.

Of course, I have been referred to as ADHD or lazy from time to time as an adult. When someone refers to me as ADHD as an adult, I'd just agree and talk about howADHD has been my hidden superpower to pursue and achieve many purpose-driven successes in my life. And when they call me lazy, I frequently just reply that I'm not lazy when I'm doing things I believe to be important for reasons greater than any individual's personal gain (including my personal gain).

For some, the discovery of their ADHD explains a lot of the frustrations they've gone through. Nick's path was a little different. Perhaps due to the memory loss of his childhood, or because of his natural optimism, Nick learned how to be self-aware and confident. That's not to say his diagnosis wasn't helpful.

When I was diagnosed, I had already gained quite a bit of self-awareness and confidence, so this really just made me a little more aware about what it might mean from a physiological perspective. It also made me more open to finding some natural treatments and strategies to position myself for success at work, such as by being very intentional about only taking on activities that lead me in a positive, purpose-driven direction.

When asked about sending his pre-diagnosed self a message, he said:

Well, I'm fortunate to not have experienced much frustration because of ADHD beforehand. I'm also a very optimistic, positive person by nature, so I didn't experience anything negative because of ADHD. And, even when people called me lazy or "ADHD," I never let it get to me for a second. So I'd just tell myself to keep pushing forward. I do value information, so I might suggest I search for a diagnosis sooner. However, I really didn't change that much after my diagnosis. It was more of a confirmation than a revelation.

Nick didn't let the label of ADHD have a negative impact on his life. He knew who he was and understood his strengths and weaknesses well. ADHD isn't the same for everyone, nor are their responses to it. Nick is a shining example of what someone can accomplish when they don't give an audience to those who would try to hold them back based on misconceptions and misunderstandings.

Productivity Problems

Your job is to cut down a huge oak tree. Your only tool is an axe from a local hardware store. Others are also tasked with cutting down oak trees, except they have chainsaws to use. You're out there every day chopping away at the tree. Long after the others have cut down their tree, you're still working on yours. Despite working from sun up to sun down, your progress is slow. How would you feel if people called you lazy for not progressing as fast as the others?

When people don't see the work you're putting into something, it's easy for them to conclude that you're lazy. It's another reason why people claim that ADHD isn't a real thing.

In their eyes, you aren't as productive because you don't want to be. They believe you're using the concept of ADHD as an excuse to be unproductive. They see you as trying to leech off others to get through life.

What they don't, or can't, comprehend is the complexity of ADHD. They need to understand how it interferes with and complicates productivity. Focus is one area that gets affected. You've likely witnessed or at least heard about kids getting super focused on their video games. "He can't pay attention in class, but he can spend hours in front of that game."

On the outside, it looks like they are avoiding responsibility and ignoring everything around them. Chores are boring. Homework is boring. Sitting around and listening to people talk is boring. If you want their attention, you have to attract their interest. It's not a conscious choice of ignoring or paying attention.

It's a matter of proper stimulation. When the brain isn't stimulated to a degree that grabs attention, it struggles to focus. You may have also noticed that sometimes they don't even pay attention to the game they're playing. A few minutes in and they want to do something else.

Many adults have learned techniques to deal with distractions and lack of interest in what they're doing. One such technique is using a Pomodoro timer. Working in short sessions allows them to focus on what they're doing while giving themselves a break to keep them interested. Many people with ADHD work on several projects on a rotation schedule to break up the monotony of boring projects.

Productivity expectations often cause stress levels to increase. Instead of being able to use their time working on various projects, their minds get overwhelmed with what others want from them. As natural people pleasers, they fight against themselves because they are not producing what they think they should. To make matters worse, many expectations are based on the production that occurs when they are hyperfocused on a project. During those times, they become so engrossed in what they're doing that they can be three to four times more productive than usual.

Let's use writing as an example. When someone with ADHD begins writing about something they enjoy, they can get engrossed and spend hours writing on the topic. All of their time and energy goes into what they're working on. That allows them to produce lengthy articles or stories in a relatively short time.

When a neurotypical person witnesses these incredible feats, they assume that it's something that always happens. When it doesn't, they attribute it to laziness. After all, hyperfocus isn't part of the Attention Deficit Hyperactivity Disorder name. They obviously don't struggle with attention deficit if they can produce that much work in that amount of time. Clearly, they have focus.

Hyperfocus is one of the traits of ADHD and not something an individual can control. The passage of time and how much work has been done doesn't occur to them until afterward. When it comes to things that aren't as interesting, the attention deficit part kicks in and they become easily distracted. Other things are more interesting for a short time, and productivity suffers.

Then, when someone hints that they might be lazy, they put more pressure on themselves to get things done. They don't want to add to the proof that they are defective. Anxiety levels go up, focus goes down, and productivity suffers. Their brains start running through everything they can, should, and need to do, and it becomes a storm of disorganization and constant slip-ups.

So Many Steps

When someone with ADHD looks at a task, they don't see one task. They see everything that goes with and around it. A normal person sees a simple list.

- Vacuum the floor

- Do the dishes

- Wash the clothes

Three simple things they can do without much effort.

People with ADHD don't see a three-item list. They see multiple sub-items within that list as well as all the steps required to finish just one item on that list. Plus, other tasks surround that one checklist item and add to the complexity of the task at hand.

➢ **Washing the dishes.**

It should be easy enough, and it is for any neurotypical person. They just have to want to do it. The person with ADHD wants to do it but also sees everything involved before they get started.

- Gather all the dirty dishes (check living room, bedrooms, kitchen counters, bathroom, back porch, front porch, garage - why are there glasses in the garage? Oh, right. I remember.)

- Make room on the counter for the overflow.

- Clean the counter to put the dishes on.

- Rinse the dishes to put in the dishwasher.

- Ugh, I have to empty the dishwasher first.

- Rearrange the cabinets so all the dishes fit - why are there so many more dishes?

- Back to the sink.

- Load the dishwasher.

A small apartment is easier to maintain because there's less distance to travel. Add going up and down stairs, down long or multiple halls, opening and closing doors, and by the time they get back to loading the dishwasher, they've lost a lot of energy and a lot of time.

> **Write that paper**

When it comes to homework or writing assignments, there's a whole world of distractions and procrastination opportunities.

- Clear off the desk so you can concentrate.

- Put the important bill somewhere so you remember to pay it.

- Turn on the computer.

- Get a drink so you don't have to get up later.

- More dirty dishes to put in the sink.

- Check notifications that popped up.

- Check email.

- Respond to email.

- Open word processing software.

- Figure out the perfect title.

- Research the web for valuable information.

- Watch that one (or one hundred) short videos.

- Focus - Focus - Focus on the paper.

- Calm the brainstorm.

- Write down everything.

- Edit everything.

- Get frustrated.

- Delete everything and start over.

- Just a quick break.

Most of it happens before anything even starts. Their minds run rampant on the processes and distractions before making that first step towards the task. There's not just one elephant to deal with. It's a stampede. One bite at a time isn't going to help.

It's not a matter of wanting to get it done; it's a problem with the motivation to get it done. The motivation has to be stronger than the torrent of insurmountable odds they see in front of them.

hyperfocus downside

Deadlines. Expectations. Desire. Stress. Interest.

At some point, ADHD switches into hyperfocus mode that tunes out every distraction. From out of nowhere comes a productivity machine that gets things done in one sitting. It's the demon and angel of the brain pushing you to the limits of accomplishments. It happens without fair warning. It happens without consideration of anything else. It doesn't care if you haven't slept well in two days or if you just woke up from a finally restful sleep. The brain forces productivity.

On the upside, a lot can be done in a short period of time. Whatever the task, the brain is on it and forces the body to comply. Dishes get done. Essays get written. The house gets cleaned. There's an extraordinary feeling of accomplishment. With it comes a dopamine rush that offers a euphoric feeling, even if it is short-lived.

The downside is how much it raises the bar of productivity expectations. It's easy to see how much was accomplished in what appears to be an effortless setting. Compare that to how much wasn't done before. You must have been lazy, holding back, procrastinating.

Is procrastination something you enjoy doing? It must be. You were capable this entire time and chose to make things more difficult. Obviously, ADHD is code for being lazy. Those with

ADHD don't need any help with comparisons of the worst kind. We know quite well how to compare our worst with another person's best. It's not only easy to beat ourselves up about it; it's second nature.

But what if it isn't laziness or intentional procrastination? What could you compare hyperfocused activity to? If you've seen any racing movies, you'll understand.

The hyperfocus aspect of ADHD is not unlike that of using NOS in a car. It gives an incredible power boost, but only for a short time. Extended use of Nitrous Oxide can destroy an engine. Extended hyperfocus can cause damage to the brain and body. How long is a safe duration of hyperfocus? It depends on the person. Whether it's twenty minutes or several hours would depend on the intensity. Lower levels of hyperfocus can go on for several hours before the brain shuts down. The basic rule is "The higher the intensity, the shorter the duration."

How long can you sprint at top speed? You might get farther on a flat straight away, but life is seldom flat, smooth or straight. How far can you swim at top speed going against the flow of a lazy river? By putting hyperfocus into that perspective, the difficulty becomes more obvious. Yes, a lot can be done in a relatively shorter period of time, but it comes at a cost.

Some might wonder why you don't always use a low level of hyperfocus. Even if it could be controlled, you wouldn't want to for the same reason you don't want to use a trickle of NOS in your car all the time. It may seem like a good thing at first, but it tears away at the components that keep the engine running smoothly. With a car, parts can be replaced. With the human brain - well, we haven't reached that level.

After a session or two of intense focus, the body and mind are exhausted. Everything hurts the next day whether you used that part of the body or not. You'll have pains in places you didn't strain. Your pectorals will be sore after a writing session. You'll have pain in your abdomen after washing dishes. Your legs will hurt like you've been on the leg press all day. Finding a direct correlation between what you did and where you hurt may not be an easy task.

When the brain goes into hyperfocus mode, it requires energy. That energy will be taken from places in the body that aren't being used or are at least being used less. The brain becomes a hoarder of energy, withholding resources from the rest of the body. The body, still being required to function, uses reserve energy until depleted. Once the resources are used up, the brain and body begin recharging. Because the body was using reserves instead of active resources, it takes longer to recover.

Lack of motivation

"Pull yourself up by your own bootstraps" is a phrase I've heard for most of my life. It never made any sense to me because it is a physically impossible task. The etymology of the phrase let me know my thinking was correct. If you don't believe it, try picking yourself up by your shoelaces and you'll get the idea.

The same can be said of motivation. Motivational speakers, gurus, psycho-ologists, managers, and even parents will tell you to be self-motivated. It's something employers used to look for in potential employees. Much like pulling yourself up by your own bootstraps, finding the means to self-motivate can be exceptionally difficult for someone with ADHD.

What motivates others doesn't motivate them in the same way. The average person finds motivation in the reward. The attention they receive for accomplishing a difficult task might be enough to get them to do more. A financial reward after a job well done motivates those seeking that reward. The NT brain recognizes rewards and seeks them out. It's the motivation they require to get things done.

The ADHD brain doesn't have the same level of dopamine production. This makes it difficult to recognize rewards and inhibits the body from acting in any particular direction. The rewards may be the same, but the ADHD brain doesn't react the same. The boost from a received reward is short-lived and, most of the time, barely makes a spike. It's seldom enough to encourage repeat actions on its own. There's no enthusiasm to be attached to the reward or to its connection to the work. That's not to say that people with ADHD don't appreciate the reward, but rather, they are limited in their ability to express their gratitude. Something else is already on their minds.

The chemical responses for showing gratitude are also responsible for recognizing and seeking rewards. Dopamine. The logical part of the brain puts the pieces together and sends the message of what is an expected and acceptable response.

- Smile.
- Say thank you.
- Show gratitude.
- Repeat the actions.

If you look into a person's eyes when you give the reward, you may not see much of a reaction. The responses are pre-programmed, but the emotions behind them are lacking. Sometimes, they may even be uncomfortable, especially if they're not used to being acknowledged. The emotional response may come later.

The vacuum cleaner works fine, but without electricity, it won't run. Think of dopamine as the electric current and the vacuum as the motivation. Trying to entice or force someone with ADHD to become motivated is like trying to get the shop vac to pick up all the dirt without plugging it in.

People with ADHD need a dopamine boost to activate their motivation. Dopamine production can come from different sources, some natural and some medicinal, but it has to be there before anything is going to happen. In some cases, the reward may have to come, at least partly, before the motivation can begin.

Seeing someone suddenly become super productive may lead you to believe it was something they could have done the whole time. That burst of productivity isn't the norm. They weren't choosing to be lazy before or procrastinate because they wanted to. Most people with ADHD hate procrastination as much as anyone, but it is a part of who they are.

The sudden motivation to get things done comes from the overwhelming build-up of stress. The release valve popped, and the result was a hyperfocused intensive output. Once that pressure has been released, the cycle starts over.

* * *

Girls Don't Have ADHD

The emergency room is crowded, as it always is on a Saturday evening with a full moon. The paramedics rush a gurney through the doors, a panic-stricken mother tight on their heels.

"What have you got?" The receiving nurse rushes to the gurney and gets the report.

"Ten-year-old patient. Ambulatory and alert. No sign of physical trauma. Heart rate eighty-five bmp. BP one-ten over sixty-eight. Breathing is normal. Mother called. Reported symptoms, hyper talkative, easily distracted, forgetful, impulsive, and showing signs of extreme shyness in public situations."

The nurse stopped, put her hands on her hips, and huffed. "Are you telling me you brought in a patient who is showing signs of ADHD? Seriously?" She gestured to the stack of people waiting for attention. "We've got more important things to deal with."

"Did I mention the patient is female?"

The nurse turned to the desk, "Contact the doctor on call, stat." She looked at the paramedics,"Put her in room eight."

The way people talk, you would think that ADHD is strictly a boy issue. It's difficult enough to dispel the idea that all boys have ADHD at some point, but it has been nearly inconceivable to convince people that girls can have ADHD as well. Assumptions have become fact in the minds of the populace, and testing girls for ADHD still seems like a foreign concept. While things have been getting better in that regard over the past few decades, it's still an uphill battle.

If a girl shows signs of ADHD, there's a sudden panic that follows. It's treated as an alien virus that will wipe out life as we know it. Suddenly, ADHD becomes an urgent issue that needs to be dealt with immediately. A cure must be found.

ADHD isn't a virus or a bacterial infection that needs to be cured. It isn't some foreign parasite or cancerous cell that needs to be extracted or bombarded with radiation. It cannot be found in blood tests or with a CT scan. It's not contagious. It's not something that wasn't there and suddenly appears. There's no such thing as "Adult ADHD" or "Sudden Onset ADHD". It doesn't care if you're male or female. It's not something restricted to a set of chromosomes.

There are, however, differences in manifestation. For the sake of simplicity, let's call them feminine and masculine traits. Both of which can be found in boys and girls alike. They're not male and female traits.

There are some differences

Why is there a stigma that boys have ADHD while girls are less likely to have it? Girls, in general, aren't tested as often as their counterparts and, therefore, are less likely to be diagnosed. The question one should ask is, Why? There's an idea that girls can't get ADHD, not that it's something to be caught. When presented with the fact that ADHD isn't something that gets transmitted like a virus, the expression changes slightly. Girls can't have ADHD. Well, that's only a little better, but still very inaccurate.

Girls, in general, display ADHD differently than boys. Parents, teachers, and even doctors are quick to test boys for ADHD based solely on their hyperactivity. Some are quick to administer medications that later prove to be unnecessary and possibly harmful. When it comes to girls, they usually attribute the signs to other things, taking each one as a separate issue and not at all connected.

If a girl is hyperactive . . .

Red lights.

Sirens.

Code red emergency.

The thought is that girls aren't supposed to be hyperactive. At least not on the outside. Most girls with ADHD don't show outward signs of hyperactivity. They do show signs of being fidgety, easily distracted, and several other indicators. Most of it goes unrecognized or as something not to be taken seriously. In many cases, the signs of ADHD in girls are shrugged off and thought of as them just being shy or trying to deal with the complications of being a girl. After all, aren't girls' minds a bit of a scramble anyway?

When you see a group of girls, they're always giggling, telling secrets, and doing girly things. It's perfectly normal. Since girls mature faster than boys, it only makes sense that their minds develop faster than their bodies. Because of that imbalance, they will seem a little odd sometimes.

Yikes! What a terrible way to dismiss the idea of girls having ADHD. Blame everything on their development and the hormones that go with it. Let's backtrack that a little. Girls can have ADHD just as easily as boys. It's not gender specific. It does, however, reveal itself in different ways.

Instead of bouncing in their seats or getting up and down frequently, a girl with ADHD may expend her energy in the form of doodling. While boys may throw the crayon, a girl is more likely to draw on her desk, hand, or clothes. Even if there's paper available. They'll cross and uncross their ankles. They'll fidget with their hair, necklace, earrings, or bracelets.

Girls with ADHD are more likely to stare out the window or get lost in a poster. Their creative minds are in a constant storytelling mode that keeps changing. Imagine short bursts of videos playing one after another. They may start talking for no apparent reason or speak faster at times than others.

Sometimes, they'll be quick with an inappropriate emotional response or have no emotional reaction at all. They may become hyper-focused on a task or assignment and not notice that their environment has changed. When engrossed, they may not have noticed the bell ringing or the other students leaving the classroom. They may still be sitting there as the next group of kids come in.

That's not to say they can't or don't show the same signs as boys. Some do. Boys, likewise, will have expressions similar to those of girls. It depends on the individual, their environment, and what they've learned to be acceptable behaviors.

Obvious differences

For the sake of simplicity and generality, there are traits that boys have and traits girls have. These traits are not exclusive to one or the other, but rather typical of one over the other.

ADHD in boys often manifests with the following behaviors:

- Hyperactive

- Anger Issues

- Inattention

- Lack of Focus

For the most part, the signs of ADHD in boys are most easily seen because they are more physical in nature.

Girls with ADHD tend to have different behavioral issues:

- Hyper Emotional

- Hyper-focused

- Daydreaming

- Hyper talkative

Some of the signs that are seen in boys with ADHD are also seen in girls. It's not a one-size-fits-all situation. Though ADHD does manifest itself differently, in general, it is prudent to look for all the various signs regardless of whether the child or adult is male or female.

A hyper-imaginative boy who may stare at nothing can also be displaying signs of ADHD. They get overlooked because it's not a typical trait for boys. A hyperactive girl could also be revealing a symptom of ADHD.

Don't jump to a diagnosis

Just as it is a bad idea to jump to conclusions, it's also a bad idea to jump to a diagnosis. One or two traits do not mean someone has ADHD.

There was a time when a boy would be seen as having ADHD simply because they were energetic. It was never revealed whether the adults couldn't handle their rambunctious behavior or just wanted a quiet environment. They jumped to the conclusion that the child had ADHD and needed to be given the proper medication to calm them down. This resulted in the zombification effect from Ritalin.

The increased effect of dopamine levels contributes to addiction-related behavior. For active children, it calmed them down but created complications, including heart-related issues, later in their lives. In those days, it didn't take much for doctors to prescribe ADHD medication. It was the popular and acceptable thing to do. Oftentimes, it was considered to be in the child's best interest, but really, it was in the immediate interest of the caregiver.

Today, the jump diagnosis is as much of a problem, if not worse. The Internet has given everyone the opportunity to look up a symptom and come to their own conclusion. Everything from a pain in the chest, a pimple in an odd place, and even mental disorders. Someone can look up the presumed issue, get caught up in the Wikinosis, and conclude that they have a particular disorder that needs to be treated.

The Internet is a hypochondriac's dream come true, giving them supporting documentation that affirms their fears.

Likewise, there are plenty of articles and documents regarding ADHD. Some good. Some not so good. Even after scrolling past the ads, viewing the first thing that pops up in an Internet search doesn't mean you've come across stable or accurate information. Every article should be confirmed with others from different sources and, if possible, from a professional.

That's also not to say that every article should be dismissed. Many are based on individual experiences or those of others with the same condition. ADHD isn't a made-up thing and can be a contributor to real-life complications.

The feminine attributes of ADHD can lead to low self-esteem, shyness, or blaming herself when things go wrong. Some may overcompensate and force themselves to become someone they aren't to fit in. That can lead to exhaustion and depression. A continual belief that they're not good enough.

The world can be a frightening place for girls with ADHD, or anyone for that matter. The constant finger-pointing that threatens to expose her so-called flaws. All she really wants to do is get away, be left alone, hide somewhere. Her shyness manifests her fear of what others think of her. Her daydreaming is an escape from the boring activity she's forced to partake in. The fidgeting is her body trying to escape into the fantasy world she's creating in her mind.

She's not being lazy or defiant. She's not broken and in need of repair. She's a girl with ADHD, and what she needs is for someone to see her for who she really is. To help her make the most of her unique abilities and train her to build the attributes that her brain isn't naturally drawn to.

Girls can have ADHD, and it's not an emergency.

* * *

It's Only Shyness

Carol usually kept to herself during the company picnics. She'd meander through the groups of people, going from one place to another without stopping anywhere for long.

"Hey Carol," her co-worker Arthur called, "you want to join us for a game of volleyball?"

She smiled and shook her head, "It's probably better that I don't," she said. "I'm horrible at sports."

Carol had a reason not to get involved with any activity. Even if she went swimming at the lake like they did last year, she stayed by the dock and just let her feet dangle in the water.

She liked people one-on-one, but groups made her nervous, anxious, and a little overwhelmed.

She's just shy

There's shy, and then there's introverted. While they may seem the same, there is a difference. Shyness is often the result of childhood experiences that instilled in a person the need to keep to themselves. It usually stems from negative influences that make a person question their validity in the world.

Oftentimes, someone is shy due to being told or shown that they don't have anything to offer. In their minds, everyone is so much better at everything. They can be fearful of speaking up because they've always been shut down. The shyness can lead to anxiety when forced to interact in settings that they are uncomfortable with. Shyness is usually a learned behavior that begins in early development. Sometimes, shyness stems from low self-esteem, a questionable view of their own self-worth, and a fear of being judged by those around them.

Introversion is a natural preference for quieter surroundings. Introverts prefer less boisterous activities and usually avoid large social settings. However, introverts can interact with other people in those settings but require some downtime to recharge. Introverts don't think less of themselves in general; they just prefer to spend time alone. People who have ADHD are often introverts, but that doesn't mean introverts have ADHD. Nor does it mean those with ADHD are naturally introverts.

Introversion, ADHD, and shyness may seem to be ingredients that all go together, but that's not necessarily the case. There's a lot more to discover when you go below the surface. The girl you think is shy may just be an introvert. She may or may not have ADHD. Having ADHD may contribute to her introversion, but that doesn't mean she's shy. Jumping to a simplistic conclusion that she's shy can lead to misconceptions on how to "fix" the problem, even if there's no problem to be fixed.

It's not a shell

It can be easy to assume that someone not as socially interactive as you'd like them to be is hiding in some shell. While everyone has a defense mechanism, keeping things to themselves is something that some people with ADHD do without thinking about it and is more readily seen in girls with ADHD. What you see as shyness might actually be a part of their internal hyperactive thought processes.

Girls with ADHD still have the desire to interact with others. They want to share their opinions, their dreams, and their ideas. They want to socialize and interact with the people around them, but an internal battle prevents them from being the social butterfly others think they should be. It's not about beauty, intelligence, or status.

Inside their minds are conversations that often don't have the opportunity to be expressed on the outside. A part of the brain physically prevents them from moving their words from their minds to their mouths. For many, writing things down is easier than speaking them out loud.

The perception of shyness is more common in girls with ADHD than it is in boys. For one thing, boys aren't allowed to be shy. Even when he's simply introverted, he gets judged for being shy and, therefore, being defective or weak. When it comes to girls being introverted, the instant conclusion is that they're shy and just need the right person to bring them out of their shells.

Girls with ADHD aren't hiding in any kind of shell. They're processing their surroundings and trying to find the best way to interact. Because of the way their minds work, they'll have entire conversations that never see the light of day.

The tendency is to try to connect the shy girl with someone outgoing and sometimes brash to make them come to life. The belief is that it's unhealthy for a girl to be alone. While this may be an outdated belief, it can still be seen by good-intentioned people who are always looking for someone they can hook them up with. It can encourage them to participate in hook-up culture, be forced to attend parties and outings, or even have a few drinks to loosen up.

The intended goal is to make them outgoing, but those intentions often backfire and cause the introverted girl to recoil. Add the impact of ADHD, and the recoil occurs faster and with more fervency. In response, the well-intended friend will try harder to connect them with a special someone to give them a sense of security and safety. The problem is that she can feel less safe when forced to interact with someone she doesn't naturally connect with.

Being an introverted girl with ADHD doesn't mean she's put up a shell to protect herself. Her natural tendency is to recharge in environments that are less stimulating. Her ADHD mind needs to have quiet places to process the bombardment of stimuli that most social situations are full of. Emotionally and intellectually, her mind needs to sort through everything and put them in their respective categories. This allows her to prepare for the next social situation and interact with those around her. You'll often find that she can have conversations with a few people with whom she finds a connection.

The conclusion may be that she's becoming less shy. The truth is, it isn't shyness that interferes with her interaction. It's the introverted ADHD brain that has been allowed to recharge and sort through things. After the interaction, she'll still need to spend some time alone to repeat the process of appearing "normal."

The right boy will fix her

Whether it's the right boy or the right girl, the idea of finding the right person to fix her shyness - which may not be shyness at all - is based on the idea that she's broken in the first place. If there is something she's struggling with, like depression or anxiety, there is no right person outside of a therapist.

Trying to fix something that isn't broken leads to frustration that can often have dire results. As it is, relationships are complicated. Forcing one based on incorrect assumptions only adds to the problem. While she may have started the relationship as an introvert, her (or his) lack of understanding of how to deal with someone with ADHD can develop into true shyness and anxiety. As time goes on, that shyness and anxiety can lead to severe depression.

The "right boy" you thought would make her more outgoing ends up pushing her deeper into her own mind. Her thoughts become a maze of mirrors that becomes more difficult to find the way out of. His frustration around her going deeper into her introversion puts more strain on the relationship. The struggles seem to become insurmountable. At best, they part ways. At worst, things can become abusive.

Mister or Miss Right

Human beings were designed for connection. That doesn't mean all connections are necessary. Many forced connections become like magnets with repelling poles trying to be stuck together. The more you force it, the more resistance you encounter.

When you see the resistance increasing, take note. It could be that the two aren't meant to make the connection you want. Making connections with other people should occur naturally. There's nothing wrong with making introductions, but once that is done, the job of the matchmaker is to step back and see if anything happens.

Everyone has a deep desire to connect with other people, even those who prefer solace, but those with ADHD can find themselves having a much more difficult time making those connections. It's not that they are resistant to the idea; it's that their minds are going in so many directions at once that it can be difficult to find enough focus to connect.

Introverted girls with ADHD are even more likely to be on the lookout for that perfect companion. They strongly desire to bond with someone willing to understand them, learn their quirks, and work with them toward a better present and future. They're also not the type to go on the hunt for that person. It's part of the "feminine" side of ADHD, keeping to themselves.

The "Masculine" side of ADHD tends to be obnoxiously outgoing until they need to take time to recharge. Both can find it difficult to settle their thoughts in order to build a relationship. That's not to say relationships don't work for those with ADHD. It simply has to occur naturally. Forcing someone to bend to the whims of a relationship just for the sake of having one is unhelpful and can be dangerous.

The best thing to do is to allow the relationship to build over time. Without allowing time for them to learn about each other and what it means to be with someone with ADHD creates situations that end in heartbreak. When those forced relationships and repeated heartbreaks occur, it leaves her with the idea that she's not right.

Not all relationships have to be romantic

The tales of forced romance gone bad can be found all over the world. Every culture, every society, and every workplace has someone who can tell you a story of their failed relationships. It usually starts with how they were pressured to be together. Who does the pressuring will vary, and the blame can be put on everyone, from parents to television. Regardless of the influencers involved, the result is always the same: bitterness and breakup.

There's also the mindset of not dating friends. The reasoning is that they don't want to ruin the connection, which is understandable to a point. Does that mean you should only date strangers? Getting into a romantic relationship with someone you just met opens the doors to more complications. And that's if you're neurotypical.

When you're neurodivergent, there are hidden issues that will come to light before long. Most NT's don't know how to deal with ND's on a deeply personal level. They'll try, but they will always know that something isn't working. The connection doesn't feel right. Both end up struggling emotionally and mentally to make the relationship work. After all, aren't they supposed to keep the romance going?

Regardless of your stance on dating or how you prefer to find that perfect someone, there has to be an understanding that romantic relationships aren't going to fix the girl with ADHD. It won't bring her out of the imaginary shell you insist she's hiding in. It's not going to make the introvert an extrovert. She can't be fixed because she's not broken. She has ADHD and processes the world in a different way than most other people. Even ND's have different ways of looking at things.

If you're looking for ways to help make her life easier and more productive, the best thing to do is find healthy ways to interact with her. Developing friendships without the intent of building a romantic relationship will help alleviate the stress and anxiety of trying to repair what isn't damaged.

Should a friendship develop into something romantic, it will have the advantage of already knowing a lot of the quirks they might have. He will better understand how to communicate with her, and she will know how he will respond to different things. If nothing romantic develops, that's fine, too. They don't have to be in a relationship that goes beyond friendship to be a source of stabilization.

She will be who she will be

There is no magical romantic relationship cure to fix her ADHD. Pushing her into a relationship with the idea that it will make her life easier is both ignorant and harmful. It is better to help her understand and accept who she is as she is. Being a social butterfly, an influencer, or a significant other to someone who is one won't change her importance. She doesn't need any of those things to be significant. Trying to force that kind of situation is more likely to push her away. Instead, take the time to understand her.

Look for ways to communicate with her that she will be receptive to. Help her communicate with you. It's not about being shy; it's about how she views the world and your reaction to her expressions of it.

She is not shy.

She is complex.

She is enough.

* * *

It's About Effort

"It's obvious to everyone but you that you're not trying hard enough. If you really wanted to find a job, you'd be out there first thing in the morning, going everywhere you can until after dark."

I did my best to suppress my anger. Do they think I'm not trying? Do they think I want to suffer financially? Fast food, warehouse, ditch digging, putting flyers on windshields. I don't care; I just need a job.

It's easy for them to talk about not trying hard enough when they can drive comfortably in their air-conditioned car from place to place. Me? I've got a bike. If it's not hot and humid, it's raining. Either way, I'm soaking wet by the time I get anywhere. And when I do show up, after drying off around the corner, I'm told to go online. They don't accept in-person applications.

That's the way things were for me multiple times in my life. No matter how hard I tried, things didn't work out. I tried every method I could to improve my situation, but nothing worked. The more I tried and failed, the more I was accused of not wanting it badly enough. The more I heard that, the more frustrated I became. After a while, I wondered what the point of it all was. No matter how much I wanted something, it wasn't going to happen.

They should try harder

Finding the right motivation isn't as easy for someone with ADHD as Neurotypical people may think. In the NT's mind, it's just a matter of trying harder. If they want it badly enough, they'll find a way. It all comes down to being motivated. For most people, motivation comes from the potential reward. Back in some mythical era of human existence, effort equaled results, and results equaled reward. There was security in knowing that efforts were appreciated and rewarded. At one time, there might have been a 1:1 ratio.

Even if that were true, that was then.

This is now.

There is no ratio

Maybe it's about luck. Maybe it is about being in the right place at the right time with the right people. Maybe it is about putting in the effort but in such a way that the right people take notice. Even Self-Made whatevers didn't do it on their own. Their efforts were rewarded by others. Without them, they wouldn't be where they are now.

No one builds a kingdom by themselves. Most Self-Made whatevers don't want you to think about that. They want you to believe all it takes is hard work and determination. They look down on those who struggle with the determination part. They indicate to anyone struggling that they should just try harder.

Even with a 1:1 ratio of effort to reward, it still wouldn't work for those with ADHD. Part of it concerns how the striatum part of the brain functions. A neurotypical brain will associate work with reward. Action with acknowledgment. When there is an association, that part of the brain lights up with activity, motivating them to do the work and put forth the effort. For the ADHD brain, that portion of the brain doesn't associate work with reward or action with acknowledgment. It lights up when the actual reward is given. Even if the logic center of the brain sees the connection, there isn't a significant enough emotional connection to offer any drive.

I'm the type of person who likes things clean and organized. My days are less stressful when there is a minimum amount of clutter. I'm more energetic when I see clear, open counters, desktops, couches, etc. Whether I'm using them or not. I feel boxed in and confined when the opposite is true. So, if I want the rewarding feelings of a neat and organized area, I would create a neat and organized area. Right? Except I don't process it that way. I see the clutter and know the work that needs to be done, but I struggle with the motivation to do it. The process to reward doesn't have a connection. I have to use other methods of motivation, some that aren't healthy, to create order out of chaos. The potential reward is as tangible as everyday trips to the moon.

Time management and procrastination

Time management is a common problem for those with ADHD. Procrastination is second nature. Tasks that don't stimulate an emotional response are left by the wayside, while tasks that are interesting in the moment get all the focus.

At some point, those uninteresting tasks need to get done, and it is usually through an emotional response that someone with ADHD is driven to do it. Until that jolt happens, there's the fine art of procrastination. Simply walking into the kitchen will reveal things for the ADHD mind to latch onto.

- I need to let the dogs out.

- I need to let the dogs in.

- I need to feed the dogs.

- Oh, look, dishes. I should probably get those washed.

- I think I heard something. Better check it out.

- There was that other thing I was supposed to do.

Even in childhood, those with ADHD find creative ways to avoid doing what they don't enjoy. Much to many parents chagrin. Even after explaining how it's better to get something done and be rid of it, the procrastination and avoidance continue. Sometimes, having a strong negative emotion tied to the avoidance feels better than doing the emotionless mundane task.

The path to success requires strategic stepping stones

It is said that failing to plan is planning to fail. At face value, that's true. It's also an easy way to dismiss the complications those with ADHD have to face every day. The process of planning is something they have to do not only every day, but throughout the day, to get anything done.

The monumental task of succeeding is inhibited by the inability to be stimulated by long-term rewards. Building and using the stepping stones to success often complicates the ability to move forward because each step is just another daunting task. They become things to do just for the sake of doing them. If those steps are viewed as mundane by a neurotypical brain, imagine how they are seen by a neurodivergent one.

The popular book, "The Slight Edge" by Jeff Olsen, offers strategies and reasons for doing a little every day. Building a future by adding one more action in the here and now. The average person struggles with implementing seemingly insignificant actions that don't seem to be taking them anywhere. They struggle with seeing the whole picture and are stuck with only the immediate in front of them. The future is some faraway galaxy that they may get to one day if everything plays out right.

The average person can motivate themselves to try harder. They can sit down and choose the path to lead them to the desired outcome. Most people don't because they get caught up in the moment. They don't have enough drive to make changes. Most people become complacent, and until that comfort level is shifted, things remain the same.

For someone with ADHD, comfort levels are always shifting, even in the established patterns they create. Something drives them to want more, and they look for ways to obtain it. They'll try different ways of motivating themselves, keeping themselves on track, and still end up on some side street in a far-off city they've never heard of. Most steps to success aren't created with the ADHD brain in mind. As hard as they try, those with ADHD find themselves unable to follow the steps. Most don't even know why.

You must not want it enough

You wouldn't tell a double-leg amputee that he can't run because he doesn't want to, and yet people are quick to assume that someone with ADHD struggles because they don't try hard enough. It's believed that if they aren't getting their desired results, it's because they don't want it bad enough. Movies, television shows, and books give the impression that all it really takes is willpower. That and happy thoughts, but mostly willpower. With enough of it, anything is possible. It really is that easy to become a success story.

Reality offers a different perspective. That's why fiction is popular. It allows an escape from reality for a while.

People with ADHD will try repeatedly to follow the prescribed methods. They will try, and fail, and try again. They're not lacking in willpower. Their own brains are working against them. They have to find sustainable processes that work for them, and that is not an easy task, especially if they don't know they have ADHD. Those repeated struggles only make it more difficult for them to see themselves as anything better than a failure. Others have done it, so why can't they? Those repeated failures drain them of any motivation.

I used to be smart

Most teenagers believe they are smarter than the adults they know. Especially their parents. It's something that is expected and is almost a right of passage. There's also a fear that one day, they'll be as dumb as those old people. As an adult, it's easy to look back and laugh. "If I knew then what I know now." For some people with ADHD, looking back at how easily school might have been makes them feel inadequate in their present circumstances. There's a reason for that.

When I was in school, I was a straight "A" student. At least until my sophomore year. Everything came crashing in at once, and I stopped caring about my grades, my family, everything. I stopped focusing on anything I was doing.

Before that, I was hyper-focused on getting my homework

done. I could sit and complete assignments using speed reading techniques and masterful skills of multi-tasking. I had to get everything done before I left school. It wasn't like I would have much chance to do any of it at home. Starting in junior high (or middle school) I worked on a shifting schedule. I would work on the assignments from the previous class while still participating at the bare minimum in the current one. My last class was usually superficial and didn't have homework. If it did, I worked on it the next morning.

When things turned upside down for me at home and school, I lost my focus. Try as I might, I couldn't really pay attention to what I was doing. It took a while, many years in fact, before I could maintain any effort for very long. A few hours a day was all I had. I gave up on having any kind of direction. I quit trying to set any goals. They didn't have any point to me anyway. I was going to fail no matter what I did.

Things became more random as I got older, and I had no sense of stability in my life. I had become used to the turmoil my life had begun to be during my sophomore year. There was no point doing anything unless it was being ready to get shifted again. I don't know if it was the shifting of my thoughts or the shifting of my life that came first, but it stayed that way for many, many years. Every new job, environment, or social connection was another shift I had to deal with, and I didn't know how. My "smarts" failed me.

A couple of decades later, I realized that my intelligence hadn't failed me. It was how my brain interprets the world around me that made things difficult. The easy steps others took, or claimed to take, weren't easy for me. They were much more complicated than they were made out to be.

I could see that there were missing pieces, but I couldn't see what those pieces were. On the rare occasions that I could talk to someone about the missing pieces, I was either dismissed as someone who was looking for excuses or as someone too stupid to understand. Occasionally, someone would listen to what I had to say, look at what I had to offer, and come to the same conclusion. While others dismissed the step-missers, a few would take consideration and rewrite or rebuild to dive deeper into what was required.

Being smart, or intelligent, or having a high IQ makes people believe that ADHD isn't something that person could have. Being those things and having ADHD leads people to the conclusion that you're just being lazy. If you're so smart, then it means you're failing because you aren't trying hard enough, or worse, because you want to.

There's more to it than trying harder

You can want, wish, strive, run, push, climb, and scramble with all your might and still not reach your goals. Slapping your arms against the waves may look like you're trying to swim, but you're really just wasting your energy. You may be trying hard to stay above water, but trying hard isn't always the best way to survive and thrive.

There are processes that everyone needs to find that work for them. Others can share their tips and tricks on what they did, but even as useful as those may be, they're never the full story. Sometimes that's intentional. Other times, it's not. Remembering every process is nearly impossible. Even people with hyperthymesia (perfect memory recall) will have some gaps, even if they're tiny.

For people with ADHD, staying on track is a difficult thing to do, especially when you're trying to do it on your own. Even more so if you're undiagnosed or untreated. That's not to say there aren't methods that can be used. The hard part is figuring out what those methods may be. It will take time, research, and determination, but it is possible.

The steps you take and the cues you use may be vastly different from what I use to help me. By finding methods that help keep you on track and moving forward, trying harder becomes trying with results. Running faster on a treadmill shows a lot of trying, but if you stay on that treadmill, you'll never climb that mountain or surf those waves.

Life can feel like a treadmill or hamster wheel—a whole lot of effort without results. Someone with ADHD has been running for a long time. They've been trying. They've been getting nowhere. It's time for them to be shown that there is other exercise equipment available. They may not know about it or how to use it. Maybe they need a rowing machine instead of a treadmill. Perhaps the elliptical is just what the mental doctor ordered.

* * *

ADHD is for Children

Candace and Steven were dismayed when they were told their son, Abel, had ADHD. For years, they kept him on the prescribed medications, which helped most of the time, but as he got older, the medications lost their efficacy. Abel's pediatrician assured them there wasn't anything to worry about. Children tend to grow out of their symptoms by their late teens, early twenties.

It was a sigh of relief when Abel graduated high school. "A few more years and he'll be fine," they thought. They even encouraged him to wean off his medication, which he did. Their relief turned to panic and anger when he still showed symptoms of ADHD well into his mid-twenties. By the time he turned thirty, they cut him off, believing he was acting out against them. They told him that when he could straighten up his life, he could come back.

Don't worry, he'll grow out of it.

Like most people, Candace and Steven believed two things. One, ADHD is an act of defiance, and two, ADHD is something that is outgrown by the time a person reaches young adulthood.

More and more adults are discovering that they have ADHD. As children, their behavior patterns and emotional ups and downs were dismissed as nothing to be concerned about. That they'll simply grow out of it. They may have been told to "grow up" or to "quit acting so childish."

As time passed, many children learned coping mechanisms and masking techniques to fit in with whatever group they were with. When it came to higher education or the workplace, they struggled to get the work done. They may have felt inadequate for not reaching the expectations others had of them. It wasn't that they weren't trying. It was their ADHD constantly getting in the way. Not knowing this, it's easy to fall into the not good enough ideology.

When someone is diagnosed as a child, it can be assumed that they'll become normal when they get older. Everything should be fine once they reach some magical age in adulthood. After all, they've been on medication for years, and they seem to be doing fine. Now that they're adults, there's no need to continue treating childhood defects. Just like teenage hormonal reactions, they've aged enough for their bodies to have grown out of the disparaging imbalance that made them act the way they did.

ADHD doesn't stop because you've reached a certain age. There's no magical number of years that makes the complications go away. Even if you've been diagnosed as a child, it doesn't mean that adulthood somehow cured you. It's a chronic condition that persists throughout your life. It may seem like you no longer have ADHD, but what has really happened is your coping mechanisms and masking have become fine-tuned enough to fool others, and possibly yourself. The symptoms may have improved, but the ADHD hasn't gone away.

According to some research, about 60% of adults still struggle with ADHD. That doesn't mean the other 40% no longer have it. They just don't struggle with the symptoms as much. Enough, at least, for them to live or appear normal. It is only the severity of the struggle that has lessened. When thrown into unfamiliar or stressful circumstances, those symptoms can come flying back with a vengeance. Most of the time, they won't understand why. There can be a shock and an "ah hah" moment when they are diagnosed or discover that they have ADHD.

There's a belief that ADHD is something made up to excuse the behavior of "boys being boys." Add to that the idea that girls can't have ADHD because they're girls, which only strengthens the stigma that it is a childhood disorder. Some people might say that they had ADHD when they were kids, but they got better. In fact, they've either learned successful coping mechanisms or they never had ADHD.

Going through life and struggling with the complications that come with having ADHD can lead to deeper issues. Depression and anxiety top the list of things someone with ADHD has to deal with daily. When asked why, they don't really have an answer.

As children, their ADHD may have been overlooked because the severity wasn't strong enough to be considered a problem. That severity grows as they get older because the issues were never addressed. They had to use willpower to get through the tough times. They were told to "man up" or "just get over it." What was once a mild case can grow into something severe that can devastate every aspect of their lives.

Superpower Backfire

There's a part of ADHD that some might call a superpower. It's that of the ability to hyper-focus. Neurotypical people don't usually display this ability even when they crack down on a particular task. For some children, this super ability allows them to excel in areas others cannot.

Their hyper-focus kicks in on the task they're working on, and the results are usually praiseworthy. This works especially well for schoolwork that interests them. Their creative, pleasure, and hyper-focused sides combine and allow them to do amazing things. It's like they slid down the bat pole and emerged fully costumed. Outside of school or other structured environments, the ability to change outfits becomes greatly impaired.

Unfortunately, the hyper-focused superpower isn't something they can control. It's a lot like those shows where someone is suddenly imbued with impressive abilities but has no idea how to control them. The hyper-focused superpower can feel like a wild animal interaction. Sometimes, it works the way you want it to, and other times it interferes.

Getting hyper-focused on a task that isn't related to anything that needs to be done can cause strife for the task-oriented individual. When the session is over, the person with ADHD will look back at all the things they should have been doing, and they will try to make up for lost time. They might even beat themselves up for it and become even less productive.

You're too old to have ADHD

The idea that ADHD is something only children have has been debunked for generations but still holds firm. Even those who accept it's not simply a childhood disorder are under the assumption that if you weren't diagnosed as a child, then you must not have it. That's like saying if you haven't been diagnosed with a sarcoma, then it doesn't exist. Turning a blind eye to something that can have a major impact on a life doesn't change the existence of it.

Those who believe ADHD is something you get during childhood often dismiss adult diagnosis. They'll see it as something made up so they can have an excuse not to be like everyone else. If your diagnosis came as an adult, then you must have suffered some kind of severe head trauma. These beliefs are ways for the neurotypicals to look down on someone, pity them, or dismiss the issues entirely. It can leave many adults with ADHD hesitant to even consider it as a factor. They'll do whatever they can to cover up their problems, and the issues will only worsen.

People can discover that they have ADHD from unrelated events. While I was being treated for seizures, nothing physical could be found for the cause. That didn't mean the seizures weren't real; it simply meant that nothing showed up in the MRI or with the E.E.G. There wasn't any noticeable brain damage or electrical stimulation that could be recorded. Still, they were severe and kept me out of any standard working environment.

Eventually, I was diagnosed with Psychogenic Non-Epileptic Seizures (PNES), and we continued to pursue treatment options. During one of the sessions, I was probably blabbering about this, that, and the other thing when I was asked if I had ADHD. Up until then, it had never been a consideration. I was given a test, and based on those results,

I began researching on my own. And I had lost the funding to be able to continue treatment.

I discovered a whole new world that explained a lot about my childhood and why I struggled so much. I was trying to succeed using the same methods neurotypical people do, but I was failing miserably. I learned that my brain doesn't see or process things the same way. I have to do things differently.

At forty-eight years old, my eyes were opened, and I had to process everything through new lenses. I spoke with a few of my siblings about some of the questions, and it turned out that I had been this way my whole life. Always different. Always sensitive. Always ADHD.

Being an adult and making this discovery, I had two choices. I could deny what was now glaringly obvious and continue trying to be what society expects me to be, or I can accept it and learn how to function in a way that benefits myself and those around me. I chose the latter.

Children who show signs of ADHD but aren't diagnosed often become the recipients of discipline that only exacerbates the issues. In my case, my mother's response to me being fidgety was for me to sit on my hands. Their generation believed that children should be seen and not heard. I was rarely heard.

Emotions were also considered to be negative. I had short-lived moments of positive emotions and was fraught with anger, frustration, anxiety, and worry, and I was always tense. I was often teased for feeling sad or depressed, whether I had a reason or not. It's because of how I was treated when any signs of ADHD came up that I learned to hide as many emotional responses as I could. I did my best to deny my emotions. At sixteen, those stuffed-down emotions became an eruption that I could not control.

Emotional dysregulation and Rejection Sensitivity Disorder, aspects of ADHD, had been an ever-present enemy my entire life. ADHD didn't hit me as an adult after some sort of trauma. Trauma aggravated other psychological issues, which led to the discovery of my ADHD. The symptoms can be traced back throughout my entire life.

It won't go away

Just as every orphan dreams that their real parents will come and get them, and that they're really wealthy and important people who had to leave them for a while, everyone with ADHD has days when they just wish it would go away. The struggles are real. That's not just a slogan for empathy or sympathy. It's a fact of everyday life.

There are days when the pressure cooker buries the needle in the red, and the only thing you can do is run, duck, and cover. There are other days when you just watch the world go by, willing but unable to participate. You wish you weren't held back by whatever wiring went wrong in your brain. Wish I may, wish I might, not have ADHD after tonight.

But ADHD doesn't go away. It's not some childhood illness that gets better over time. There's no magic pill to make things all better, and there's no hypnotherapy option to make it go away. There are, however, treatments and strategies to make it so that ADHD doesn't exist as a hindrance.

When the diagnosis comes later in life, choices have to be made. Accept it, learn how others have managed to move forward or deny it, and continue working the way you always have. Coping mechanisms and masking techniques have worked for a lot of people with ADHD. That doesn't mean they don't come with dangerous side effects. Something is going to suffer and suffer badly.

Learning to work with your ADHD, taking medications if necessary, doesn't mean it will go away. It will always be there, just as it has been your entire life. Looking back, you may recognize the symptoms from your childhood even if you don't recognize them as being there as an adult. What changed is how you compensated for the struggles.

You may have discovered, like I have, that the night allows me to be more creative while the day allows me to be more logical and strategic. Some parts of your mind work better at certain times of the day, depending on the task that needs to be completed. You may discover that the career or lifestyle draining your energy could use a mild shift. That slight shift could make all the difference.

ADHD isn't going to go away. It's not going to vanish like the morning fog. That doesn't mean you have to stumble around with no direction. Accepting that it is a part of you is the first step in learning how to live and thrive with it.

* * *

Intelligence Makes No Difference

"I could have been in Mensa" is a statement that is often laughed at by people who are members. Their membership affords them a certain amount of arrogance. Of course, that comes at a cost.

There are those who qualify for Mensa that don't join for one reason or another. There are also those who qualify who struggle with ADHD. Trying to rationalize the constant struggle with working memory, immediate recall, and a dozen other things with having a recorded high I.Q. can make your head spin. Shouldn't an intelligent person be able to beat the ADHD problem?

Somehow, the idea of intelligence being related to ADHD has permeated the minds of a lot of people. If a child does well in school, it's not even a consideration to test them for ADHD. After all, people with ADHD fall well below the average Intelligence Quotient.

If they're given an IQ test and perform well but still have other issues or show signs of ADHD, then there must be something else going on. Perhaps it's a matter of discipline, shyness, laziness, or they're just not trying hard enough. After all, an intelligent person can eliminate their ADHD if they put their minds to it. It's impossible to be a high achiever if you have ADHD, and you can't have ADHD if you're highly intelligent.

The origins and supporting evidence that people with ADHD are of lower intelligence may come from the way we view intelligence. Some people put a lot of emphasis on an IQ score and hold on to that number as though it will magically open doors for them. In some circles, it may. Like being a part of Mensa or something of that nature. A high IQ doesn't guarantee success and can often be a source of frustration for those with ADHD and a high IQ.

Others emphasized school performance. If you take good

notes, participate in class, and get good grades, then you have the makings of a successful person. People with ADHD often struggle with those aspects and are looked down on as being unintelligent. A conundrum is seen when the low-performing student scores high on an IQ test. Clearly, they have the intelligence others admire, yet they struggle to perform the simple day-to-day tasks required of them. How can that be? Surely, it's not from ADHD.

ADHD doesn't impact a person's intelligence levels, but it does impact how they process and express information. Noted physicist Albert Einstein is known for not fitting in with those around him. His ideas were wild. His calculations were out of this world. His IQ is believed to be 160. Some consider that to be genius level. Some standards say anything over 140 is considered a genius. Since there's no record of him taking an IQ test, we can only estimate.

However, we do know that he made history. One thing that they don't teach in school is that Albert Einstein had ADHD. He didn't do so well in academia or social circles. His mind worked differently, not deficiently. He's not the only one, either.

Alexander Graham Bell is noted as having a 180 IQ. If you don't know anything about him, well, I suggest phoning a friend for some information. He, too, is said to have ADHD. Agatha Christie, John Lennon, George Bernard Shaw, Jules Verne, and many others throughout history are considered to have been highly intelligent and showed signs of ADHD. We can include John F. Kennedy, with an IQ of 159.8, and Leonardo da Vinci, with an estimated IQ between 180 & 220, to that list as well. What we know of the signs of ADHD can be traced in their lives.

ADHD doesn't mean dumb

Imagine if all the people in the world who had ADHD were actually imbeciles, having low intelligence or intelligence equivalent to that of an average 3-7-year-old. Can you picture how many people you know would be completely different from what you know of them now? A simple internet search can lead you to a long list of celebrities, inventors, and musicians who have ADHD. Imagine all the people living with ADHD being simpletons. The world would be a much different place.

It's not just academia that can be problematic for people with ADHD and cause others to think of them as less intelligent. It's also within social environments. It's not uncommon for them to say something that seems so unrelated as to be nonsense. In their minds, they see the connections. Sometimes, they can explain those connections, but other times, they're shut down before they get the chance. They get dismissed as being idiotic because the other people can't see what they see. Others may be able to make the connection but don't like what they think they're hearing.

It's easier to dismiss an off-the-wall comment than it is to try and understand it. This can lead to the ADHD'er to shut down and not participate. If other people don't want to hear what they have to say, then why say anything at all?

Problem solvers. Creative thinking. Solution makers. These are the things that make someone with ADHD valuable. Not their test scores or social interactions. Oftentimes, their intelligence goes unnoticed because those around them have closed their eyes. They want things done the way they've always been done.

People with ADHD think outside the box, and in most circles, that can be a frightening thing. Neurotypicals claim they want people who do exactly that but then can't accept the new ideas. It makes them look or feel bad, and they retaliate by calling the other person names. Degrading someone, then taking their ideas and passing them off as their own is easier for them to deal with than accepting that someone with ADHD might be a little brighter.

Intelligence can hide ADHD
One of the struggles with ADHD is executive function. The

ability to plan, focus, self-regulate, remember, etc. For most neurotypicals, these aspects of life come easily. Self-help coaches tout the importance and simplicity of planning a person's day, week, month, year. All you have to do is. . . whatever it is they recommend. Get a calendar. Write down specific events. Create a journal. These seem like simple enough tasks, but for someone with ADHD, these can be sheer cliff faces that are impossible to climb.

Not everyone with ADHD has the same struggle with executive function. Some have discovered ways that work for them to overcome the complications that others have not. They can take their moments of hyper-focus and create guides that allow them to become high achievers.

Additionally, ADHD manifests itself differently in those with high IQs. Because of the way people with high intelligence process information, those with ADHD have a reasonably easier time bypassing the connections that aren't working and compensating through other methods.

It may seem like those with higher intelligence levels have overcome or managed to get rid of their ADHD symptoms, but the reality is they've learned to mask it. There's a constant rerouting going on. The detours are always changing. The compensation is ongoing. Rather than being able to build a new highway, their brains are repeatedly building new bypasses. Like the stairway structures of an M C Escher painting or the movie version of it in "Labyrinth". What worked last time has already been torn down to build a new one for a new issue. Another one has to be rebuilt to solve the previous problem.

As the brain ages, as is the case for most brains, the ability to rehash new constructs begins to slow, even for those under constant mental stimulation. The slowing process can lead to more stress and frustration, which in turn reveals the ADHD symptoms. Some subscribe to "Adult-onset ADHD." In those cases, it is likely that the coping and masking mechanisms they've relied on for most of their lives have begun to fall apart. The hidden reality of their ADHD has started to come to light.

A child who does well in school, gets good grades, is great at problem-solving, and is discovered to have a higher-than-average IQ may not be a consideration for ADHD testing. They not only manage to get their book reports done on time, but usually early. In addition, their reports are well-written and insightful, covering everything on the checklist. The same goes for their homework. While average students complete their assignments on time, they pass with nothing exceptional to say about it. Does that mean the student who seems to be doing well doesn't have ADHD? Not necessarily.

No truly comparative tests have been conducted between highly intelligent neurotypicals and highly intelligent neurodivergents. The high IQ ADHD student can look at a task, focus on it, and use various coping mechanisms they may not be aware of to complete the assignment with little to no complications, especially if it interests them. However, they are less likely to remain focused on that assignment or grade. The momentary reward of praise is fleeting, and their minds are racing off to the next thing.

From the outside, it seems like they don't care. Essentially, they don't. They need that reward, but the gratification of it is short-lived. They are often the ones who don't live in the "Glory Days" because there is a lack of emotional connection between what was and what is. They are more likely to dwell on the areas where they didn't live up to their own expectations.

Remove the perceived connection

When you remove intelligence as a factor for determining whether or not someone has ADHD, you can begin to see the other symptoms. The IQ level of an individual isn't a symptom or result of ADHD. The two are not related. People who look at a child or an adult, and consider them to be intelligent should accept that level of intelligence as something that stands on its own.

Some people with what some consider to be genius-level IQs struggle with what direction they want to take their lives. Most people are good at one or two things. They find themselves passionate about one or two things. If they're fortunate, what they enjoy and what they're good at will coincide. That applies to people with and without ADHD.

For the highly intelligent individual with ADHD, they may discover that they are good at a lot of different things. Unrelated things. They can be passionate about opposite things and be good at both. Their choices for where they want to go in life become overwhelming. Too many forks in the road, and all the roads have been well traveled.

Not knowing what direction to take, they may not decide at all and try to allow life to decide. It's not that they don't have any drive; it's that their drive is going in too many directions at once. Their intelligence demands they learn more. Their ADHD demands that a decision be made, but they can't make one. Their passion wants to taste everything at the buffet.

If they can afford it, they may become perpetual students—always learning, taking different courses, and using what they can to earn more money, grants, and scholarships. Academia becomes a safe place where they can feed their intellect and their fluctuating passions without having to settle for any one thing.

If they can't afford it, well, it's off to the job boards and lower-level employment options. Their resumes are filled with jobs that don't build on the previous ones. Fast food, network troubleshooter, coder, writer, customer service, warehouse worker, construction, and security specialist. A hodgepodge of jobs without any clear focus or direction.

To look at a CV like that, one might assume that the person lacks intelligence. However, at each job, they were known for climbing the ladder fast. Then they got bored. Their direction changed. Their minds starved for something else. They moved on. It wasn't their intelligence that was lacking but rather their ADHD, keeping them from focusing on one thing. Their minds required - no, demanded - something new.

People with ADHD are no more prone to be intelligent or unintelligent than neurotypicals. It may seem that way from how society portrays them based on limited information and a willingness to understand. They can have genius-level intelligence, average intelligence, and below-average intelligence. ADHD doesn't care about that. It wants what it wants, and it isn't even sure what that is.

The only real part intelligence levels play is in how the ADHD is masked and compensated for, sometimes to the detriment of the individual.

* * *

All ADHD is the Same

People with ADHD can relate to each other in a lot of different ways. For example, disliking certain foods because of the texture isn't uncommon. The particular foods differ from person to person. When I was young, I refused to eat meat. No chicken. No beef. No pork. I hated it. It had nothing to do with a cry against cruelty to animals or because I thought being a vegetarian was better for you. Nope, it was because I couldn't handle the texture.

Being easily distracted is another relatable issue, though the ease of that distraction won't be the same for you as it is for me, nor will it be the same in most situations. Then there's the hyper-focus issue. What interests one person may bore another. One person could sit and read the encyclopedia in hardcopy all day while another doesn't want to touch the paper or have any interest in what Brittanica has to say.

People who know someone with ADHD may think they know everything there is to know. The truth is, even people with ADHD learn new things from others with ADHD.

Two Charlies

Charlie sat at the back of the class every day. It was her favorite place to sit, away from her clamoring classmates. There, she could sit in peace without the fear of getting called on by the teacher. The teacher had thirty-plus other students she could call on, and it was rare she would expel much energy looking to the back of the class, especially since there were other students in front of her who were more than willing to participate.

Charlie would read the class material but wasn't very good at taking notes. What good were notes anyway if she couldn't use them during a test? Without knowing what questions would be on the test, writing down anything specific didn't make sense. She'd just have to read and re-read the material until she could make sense of it. Tests weren't about understanding the material; they were about what you could memorize.

One day, Charlie felt her heart racing as the teacher called her name. She froze, stared into the void, and hoped that she could disappear. She hadn't even heard the question, and she could forget about answering it correctly.

Even when she realized that the teacher was calling on a different Charlie, a boy in her class who was always eager to answer, her anxiety followed her all the way home and past dinner. Her parents didn't ask any questions. They couldn't care less. They ate in silence, and she spent the rest of the night in her room reading the class material. Charlie has undiagnosed ADHD and suffers from anxiety daily.

The other Charlie, the one eager to answer questions, sits next to the window. He doesn't like to be surrounded by people, and the window view allows him to escape, mentally if not physically. When the class gets too loud, and he feels a bit distant, he'll stare out the window and imagine himself out in the field. His mind can relax and forget the tension his body is feeling.

That Charlie likes to answer questions. He wants his teacher to notice him and praise him for anything he does right. Over the years, he's learned to be wary of the looks the other students give him and is very careful not to answer too many questions. He learned to avoid getting punched in the face for making others look bad.

He needs the teacher's positive attention. She was kind, and those simple words "that's correct" meant the world to him. He avoided answering questions he wasn't one hundred percent sure of because the risk of being wrong was too much. One incorrect answer, and he'd spend the rest of the night making sure he didn't make another mistake.

He had to be perfect in everything he did or face punishment from his parents. He knew he'd never be good enough for them to love him, but he had to try just the same. He knew his classmates would always hate him, but he did what he could to fit in without making a stir.

This Charlie also has ADHD and anxiety disorder.

Both Charlies have ADHD, neither of which will be discovered for years after they graduate. They not only share the same name but also the same disorder. Their outward appearances couldn't be more different. Their outward actions, or rather reactions, to external situations are also vastly different.

The first Charlie tries to avoid social contact in any way she can. All she wants to do is get through the school day and spend time by herself. Outside the safety of her room, everything is too bright, too loud, too intrusive. She can feel the judgment in the eyes of anyone looking at her, including her parents. If she can't be good enough to be accepted, she'd rather be invisible. It's not worth trying to be a part of anyone else's world.

The second Charlie does everything he can to fit in. He doesn't want to be ignored or overlooked. At the same time, he doesn't want to let anyone down. Whether they accept him or not is entirely up to him. He has to make friends with people and refuses to turn anyone away. No matter what they ask of him. If it gets them to be his friend, he'll do it. He's learned when to participate in class and when not to. When things get too much, and he feels his emotions getting too strong, he drifts away in his mind. He can't allow himself to have emotions that may push someone away. Only the right responses are acceptable to him because if he's ever wrong about something, his friends and family will leave.

Common but different

If you have ADHD or know someone else who does, odds are you've been confronted with the comparative conundrum. It often comes from those who believe their knowledge and understanding of ADHD is the ultimate resource. They may have known someone from childhood who had ADHD and can tell you all about it. Every aspect and response that person had. In their minds, it has become the scale by which everyone else is measured.

When someone with ADHD doesn't fit into their prescribed response categories, they don't consider them to have ADHD. There must be something else wrong with them.

> *"My friend's son has ADHD. You have to repeat yourself all the time if you want him to do something. People with ADHD just don't pay attention. They're unreliable."*

> *"My cousin's daughter was diagnosed with ADHD. Ever since they put her on those pills, she's been like a zombie. I think they just wanted to drug her up so she wouldn't be so annoying. Before them, she never shut up. Of course, that was only around the family. Take her to the park, and she'd just sit there by herself and ignore everyone. She was a very rude child."*

> *"You're outgoing and smart; you can't have ADHD. I see you interacting with people all the time. My Timmy has ADHD, and he's nothing like that. He barely gets by in school. You don't have ADHD."*

Everyone with ADHD has some things in common with everyone else with ADHD. If not, there wouldn't be recognizable symptoms to make a diagnosis. Having something in common with another person doesn't mean you're exactly alike.

Not everyone with ADHD struggles with Rejection Sensitivity Dysphoria. Not everyone with ADHD has severe emotional dysregulation. Some people with ADHD have learned to act like everyone else. That doesn't mean they don't struggle on the inside and in private.

Environment alters expression
Some children are encouraged to speak their minds, act out

their impulses, and express their emotions however inclined. That encouragement may not come so much in the way of words. Others are discouraged from any kind of expression unless it makes their parents look good. The internal struggle and lack of understanding of how to express themselves in a "positive" way causes them to not express themselves at all. Sometimes, the emotions explode, as they tend to do for those who have ADHD, and instead of trying to understand the explosion, the child is simply punished or ignored.

The first Charlie's parents' silence about how her day went or how she felt sent her a clear message that they didn't care. They weren't interested in her feelings, her anxiety, or anything that happened to her. The message she received was to keep quiet. If her parents didn't want to talk about it, why should she?

The second Charlie had parents who seemed eager to find anything wrong with his behavior. They weren't so much interested in what he did as they were in the results he received. Did he get good grades? Were the comments on his report card affirmations or condemnations? Their interests were in how they could find reasons to punish him. At least, that's his perspective. His focus turned to pleasing people to avoid punishment, even at the risk of losing the rewards of affirmation.

Another child runs up and down the aisles of the store, stopping now and again to play with a toy he sees. It has a button that says "Try Me," and he has to push that button. Sometimes, it plays or moves in a way that grabs his attention, and when it stops, he has to push it again. When he gets bored with that one, there's another one he can try. And another. And another. There becomes an impulsion that prevents him from not pushing the button. (*Even at my age, I have to resist the urge to push the button. I don't always succeed.*)

On the aisles where there are no toys, there are other things that can grab his attention. A brightly colored box. A ball. Those hanging clips with the impulse buy items. He might grab several items, walk around with them for a while, and then leave them in random places without thinking. All the while, his parents do nothing to keep him from moving or opening anything. When he gets excited, he might squeal with delight. When he gets upset because something doesn't respond the way he wants it to, he might scream his frustration. The parent, ignoring his behavior, sends the message that it's acceptable.

Severity Spectrum

The complexity of ADHD can make it difficult to understand and diagnose. Some children with ADHD become performance-driven, while others can be defiance-driven. Some can display both, depending on their environment. Some may struggle with inattention, disorganization, and lack of impulse control. They jump from one topic to another, work on one project for a short while, and move on to another without completing the first. Most of the time, the focus lasts for about fifteen to thirty minutes on good days, but can be as short as two or three minutes.

They tend to lose things quickly, especially if they haven't learned organizational skills. They had the pencil a second ago, set it down, picked up something else, and now can't find the pencil. The larger the space to keep something, the easier it is for them to lose it. They may walk across the living room with the phone and return without it. A half-hour may pass before they realize it's not in their pocket, and they'll go looking for it.

Some people with ADHD may display a high level of defiant disorder. They have a problem with authority or authoritative behavior. Being told what to do grates against their neurons, and they respond defiantly. In some cases, it can be extreme and, depending on the circumstances, threatening.

Others may not appear to have the same defiant disorder because it doesn't manifest in a way that is obvious to the casual onlooker. They may do as they are told, but do so with the bare minimum of effort. However, when asked, not ordered, to do the same task, their brains respond differently. Not only will they complete the task they requested, but they will also go above and beyond.

When it comes to social interactions, you can find people with ADHD being, or trying to be, the center of attention. They want all eyes and ears on them. They need the affirmations of attention, even if it requires them to do or say something harmful or hurtful. What they do or say is irrelevant to them as long as they get the attention they seek. The environment in which they were raised will determine how far in either direction they will go.

You'll also find people with ADHD being more reclusive. They may give short answers, casual nods, or avoid eye contact. It's not that they don't like anyone there, but they would rather avoid attention except for a select few. Even then, if others are around, they may not be able to get themselves to open up.

ADHD affects those who have it in different ways. Even when exposed to the same environmental and cultural influences, no two people will have the same expressions or share the same degree of symptoms. For some, the effects are mild, while in others, they can be severe.

There are also emotional and physical conditions that will have an impact on the outward appearance of ADHD. There can be times when they may fall into a deep state of depression without understanding why, or they may feel a momentary exhilaration of excitement for something that others would consider mundane. It can be a roller coaster of each individual's emotions, expressions, and behavior.

To assume that someone doesn't or can't have ADHD because they aren't like someone else with the same condition is to have a complete misunderstanding of ADHD. It is not accurate or helpful to make assumptions about a person with ADHD based on stereotypes or generalizations.

To truly understand someone with ADHD, you have to get to

know the individual. Everyone is different, and your willingness to not come to broad-stroke conclusions will allow you to learn directly from those who would otherwise shut you out.

* * *

Acknowledgments:

Special thanks to the following people and groups who have made this book possible through their stories, assistance, and encouragements.

The Prosperous Writer Group on Facebook

Rick Fordyce - Editor

Brigitte Cutshall - Proofreader

Kent Sanders, Nick Pavlidis, Nathan Whitbread: My wonderful interview victims

* * *

About the Author

Micheal is a Neurodivergent Ghostwriter and Eclectic Author who works in Fiction and Non-Fiction. He has experience with ADHD, Schizo-Affective Disorder, Conversion Disorder, and more. As a late-diagnosed neurodivergent, Micheal has had to come face to face with the realities, difficulties, and advantages that are related to Attention Deficit Hyperactivity Disorder. He is certified in 'Unlocking Your Potential with ADHD.'

With a background in engineering, health care, technical support, customer service, and communications, he brings an array of experiences and skills to his writing and creative work.
Micheal is also passionate about travel and meeting new people. He was born with a crayon and a piece of paper in his hand and is always looking for his next adventure.